First World War
and Army of Occupation
War Diary
France, Belgium and Germany

23 DIVISION
68 Infantry Brigade
Northumberland Fusiliers
10th Battalion
25 August 1915 - 31 October 1917

WO95/2182/3

The Naval & Military Press Ltd
www.nmarchive.com
Published in association with The National Archives

Published by

The Naval & Military Press Ltd

Unit 10 Ridgewood Industrial Park,

Uckfield, East Sussex,

TN22 5QE England

Tel: +44 (0) 1825 749494

www.naval-military-press.com

www.nmarchive.com

This diary has been reprinted in facsimile from the original. Any imperfections are inevitably reproduced and the quality may fall short of modern type and cartographic standards.

© **Crown Copyright**
Images reproduced by permission of The National Archives, London, England, 2015.

Contents

Document type	Place/Title	Date From	Date To
Heading	WO95/2182/3 10 Bn N'berland Fus Aug 1915-Oct 1917		
Miscellaneous	23rd Division 68th Infy Bde 10th Bn North'D Fus. Aug 1915-1917 Oct To Italy.		
Heading	10th North Fus. Jany-Dec 1916		
Heading	German Accounts Battle Of Le Cateau.		
Heading	23rd Divn 10th Northumb. Fus. Vol I Aug & Sept 15. Feb 19		
War Diary	Bramshott	25/08/1915	25/08/1915
War Diary	Folkestone	25/08/1915	25/08/1915
War Diary	Boulogne	25/08/1915	25/08/1915
War Diary	Pont De Brigade Station Boulogne	26/08/1915	26/08/1915
War Diary	Watten	26/08/1915	26/08/1915
War Diary	Ganspette.	27/08/1915	06/09/1915
War Diary	Hazebrouck.	07/09/1915	07/09/1915
War Diary	S Of Bailleul	08/09/1915	09/09/1915
War Diary	Trenches	10/09/1915	10/09/1915
War Diary	Lesantie	11/09/1915	11/09/1915
War Diary	Trenches	12/09/1915	12/09/1915
War Diary	Lesantie	13/09/1915	13/09/1915
War Diary	Trenches	14/09/1915	14/09/1915
War Diary	Lesantie	15/09/1915	15/09/1915
War Diary	Bivonack	16/09/1915	17/09/1915
War Diary	Jesus Farm	18/09/1915	26/09/1915
War Diary	Estaires	27/09/1915	27/09/1915
War Diary	Jesus Farm.	28/09/1915	28/09/1915
War Diary	Estaires	29/09/1915	01/10/1915
Heading	23rd Division 10th Northumberland Fus: Vol 2 Oct 15 121/7595		
War Diary	Estaires	02/10/1915	02/10/1915
War Diary	1st Line Trenches	03/10/1915	06/10/1915
War Diary	Support Trenches & Billets	07/10/1915	10/10/1915
War Diary	Frost Trenches	12/10/1915	15/10/1915
War Diary	'A' Trenches	16/10/1915	16/10/1915
War Diary	'D' Position	17/10/1915	20/10/1915
War Diary	'A' Trenches	21/10/1915	25/10/1915
War Diary	'C' Position	26/10/1915	29/10/1915
War Diary	'A' Trenches	30/10/1915	31/10/1915
Heading	23rd Division 10th Northumb: Fus: Vol:3 121/7761 Nov 15		
War Diary	'A' Trenches	01/11/1915	02/11/1915
War Diary	Jesus Farm	03/11/1915	08/11/1915
War Diary	D Position	09/11/1915	10/11/1915
War Diary	A Position	11/11/1915	13/11/1915
War Diary	C Position	14/11/1915	17/11/1915
War Diary	Jesus Farm	18/11/1915	24/11/1915
War Diary	Left Sector A Position	25/11/1915	28/11/1915
War Diary	D Position	29/11/1915	02/12/1915
War Diary	A Position	03/12/1915	05/12/1915
Heading	23rd Div Raid Night Of 31st Dec/1st Jan		

War Diary	A Position	06/12/1915	06/12/1915
War Diary	C Position	07/12/1915	14/12/1915
War Diary	Rue Dormoire	15/12/1915	22/12/1915
War Diary	D Position Right Sector	22/12/1915	30/12/1915
War Diary	'C' Position Right Sector	31/12/1915	01/01/1916
War Diary	'C' Position	02/01/1916	04/01/1916
Heading	10th Northumb: Fus: Vol:5 23rd		
War Diary	C Position Right Sector	05/01/1916	07/01/1916
War Diary	Jesus Farm.	08/01/1916	15/01/1916
War Diary	Rue Marle	16/01/1916	19/01/1916
War Diary	A Position Left Sector.	20/01/1916	23/01/1916
War Diary	C Position Left Sector	24/01/1916	27/01/1916
War Diary	A Position Left Sector	28/01/1916	31/01/1916
War Diary	Rue Dormoire	31/01/1916	08/02/1916
War Diary	Rolanderie Farm	09/02/1916	12/02/1916
War Diary	B Position Right Sector	13/02/1916	17/02/1916
War Diary	Rue Delettre	18/02/1916	21/02/1916
War Diary	Jesus Farm	22/02/1916	25/02/1916
War Diary	Bac St Maur	26/02/1916	26/02/1916
War Diary	Morbecque	27/02/1916	29/02/1916
War Diary	Marnes Les Mines.	01/03/1916	08/03/1916
War Diary	Verdrel	09/03/1916	16/03/1916
War Diary	Hersin.	17/03/1916	17/03/1916
War Diary	A Position Calonne Sector.	18/03/1916	21/03/1916
War Diary	Bully.	22/03/1916	25/03/1916
War Diary	A Position Calonne Sector.	26/03/1916	29/03/1916
War Diary	C Position Calonne Sector.	30/03/1916	02/04/1916
Miscellaneous	A.G. Base Herewith The War Diary Of The 10th North Fusiliers for The Month Of April 1916	01/05/1916	01/05/1916
War Diary	A Position Calonne Sector.	03/04/1916	06/04/1916
War Diary	D Position Bully.	07/04/1916	10/04/1916
War Diary	'A' Position Calonne Sector.	11/04/1916	15/04/1916
War Diary	C Position Calonne.	16/04/1916	18/04/1916
War Diary	Hersin.	19/04/1916	26/04/1916
War Diary	Divion.	27/04/1916	30/04/1916
Miscellaneous	A.G. 3rd Echelon Herewith Is The War Diary Of The 10 Northd Fus For The Month Of May 1916	06/06/1916	06/06/1916
War Diary	Divion.	01/05/1916	20/05/1916
War Diary	Souchez. I	21/05/1916	25/05/1916
War Diary	Notre Dame Defence "C" Position.	26/05/1916	31/05/1916
War Diary	Souchey I	01/06/1916	04/06/1916
War Diary	D Position Novlette Wood.	05/06/1916	09/06/1916
War Diary	D Position Reserve Verorel.	09/06/1916	10/06/1916
War Diary	Dieval	11/06/1916	11/06/1916
War Diary	Crepy	12/06/1916	14/06/1916
War Diary	Dennebroeucq	15/06/1916	24/06/1916
War Diary	Picquigny	25/06/1916	30/06/1916
Miscellaneous	68th Inf. Bde. 23rd Div. War Diary 10th Battn. The Northumberland Fusiliers. July 1916		
War Diary	Roulainville	01/07/1916	01/07/1916
War Diary	Franvillers	02/07/1916	02/07/1916
War Diary	Millencourt	03/07/1916	03/07/1916
War Diary	Trenches Reserve Albert.	03/07/1916	04/07/1916
War Diary	Becourt	04/07/1916	04/07/1916
War Diary	Reserve Trenches Nr Albert.	04/07/1916	05/07/1916
War Diary	Becourt Wood.	05/07/1916	06/07/1916

War Diary	Scotts Redoubt	06/07/1916	10/07/1916
War Diary	Becourt.	10/07/1916	10/07/1916
War Diary	Albert.	10/07/1916	15/07/1916
War Diary	Usna-Tara Reserve Line.	15/07/1916	17/07/1916
War Diary	Near Pozieres	18/07/1916	18/07/1916
War Diary	Trenches Near Pozieres	18/07/1916	20/07/1916
War Diary	Franvillers.	21/07/1916	26/07/1916
War Diary	Bivonac Nr Albert.	26/07/1916	26/07/1916
War Diary	Trenches Between Pozieres and Bazentin-Le-Petit.	26/07/1916	27/07/1916
War Diary	Trenches	27/07/1916	28/07/1916
War Diary	Albert.	28/07/1916	31/07/1916
Miscellaneous	68th Brigade. 23rd Division. 1/10th Battalion Northumberland Fusiliers August 1916 Report On Raid 30/31st.		
War Diary	Albert	01/08/1916	01/08/1916
War Diary	Contalmaison.	01/08/1916	03/08/1916
War Diary	Trenches	03/08/1916	04/08/1916
War Diary	Contalmaison	04/08/1916	05/08/1916
War Diary	Albert.	05/08/1916	06/08/1916
War Diary	Tara Valley	07/08/1916	08/08/1916
War Diary	Lahoussoye	08/08/1916	11/08/1916
War Diary	Gorenflos.	12/08/1916	13/08/1916
War Diary	Fletre. W.5.a.3.6. Billets:	13/08/1916	14/08/1916
War Diary	Steenwerck	15/08/1916	15/08/1916
War Diary	Le Bizet.	16/08/1916	16/08/1916
War Diary	Left Subsector Right Sector Le Tooques Trenches.	17/08/1916	24/08/1916
War Diary	D Position Armentieres & Le Bizet	25/08/1916	31/08/1916
Operation(al) Order(s)	Minor Operation Order No. 62	29/08/1916	29/08/1916
Miscellaneous	Account Of Raid Carried Out On Night Of 30/31 August '16	30/08/1916	30/08/1916
Diagram etc			
War Diary	Armentieres.	01/09/1916	03/09/1916
War Diary	Bailleul	04/09/1916	04/09/1916
War Diary	Courte Croix.	05/09/1916	10/09/1916
War Diary	Molliens Au. Bois.	11/09/1916	11/09/1916
War Diary	Millencourt	12/09/1916	15/09/1916
War Diary	Becourt.	16/09/1916	17/09/1916
War Diary	O.G.I. Near Villawood.	18/09/1916	19/09/1916
War Diary	Peake Wood.	20/09/1916	21/09/1916
War Diary	O.G.1	22/09/1916	22/09/1916
War Diary	B Position Martinpuich	23/09/1916	25/09/1916
War Diary	C Position	26/09/1916	26/09/1916
War Diary	Scotts Redoubt	27/09/1916	30/09/1916
Miscellaneous	Account Of Attack On 25th September 1916	25/09/1916	25/09/1916
War Diary	Scotts Redoubt	01/10/1916	02/10/1916
War Diary	Shelter Wood	03/10/1916	03/10/1916
War Diary	A Position Le Sars.	03/10/1916	06/10/1916
War Diary	D Position	07/10/1916	08/10/1916
War Diary	Becourt.	09/10/1916	11/10/1916
War Diary	Gorenflos	12/10/1916	12/10/1916
War Diary	Oneux.	13/10/1916	14/10/1916
War Diary	Laurence Camp.	14/10/1916	16/10/1916
War Diary	Ypres	17/10/1916	18/10/1916
War Diary	A Position Trenches	19/10/1916	20/10/1916
War Diary	D Position Ypres	21/10/1916	23/10/1916
War Diary	Poperinghe.	24/10/1916	29/10/1916

Type	Description	From	To
War Diary	A Position Right Sector.	30/10/1916	31/10/1916
Miscellaneous	10th Northumberland Fusiliers. Training Programme.	22/10/1916	22/10/1916
War Diary	A Position Right Sector Trenches.	01/11/1916	02/11/1916
War Diary	D Position Rt. Sector Ypres	03/11/1916	06/11/1916
War Diary	A Position Right Sector Trenches	07/11/1916	10/11/1916
War Diary	St. Lawrence Camp	11/11/1916	16/11/1916
War Diary	C. Position Left Sector Ypres Barracks	17/11/1916	20/11/1916
War Diary	A Position Left Sector	21/11/1916	24/11/1916
War Diary	D Position Ypres Barracks	25/11/1916	29/11/1916
War Diary	Reserve St Lawrence Camp	30/11/1916	30/11/1916
War Diary	St Lawrence Camp.	01/12/1916	01/12/1916
War Diary	Corps Reserve Position.	07/12/1916	07/12/1916
War Diary	A Position Right Sector.	07/12/1916	11/12/1916
War Diary	C Pos. Zillebeke Bund.	11/12/1916	16/12/1916
War Diary	A Position Rudkin House	17/12/1916	20/12/1916
War Diary	D Position Ypres.	21/12/1916	23/12/1916
War Diary	D Position Hospice Ypres.	21/12/1916	23/12/1916
War Diary	St Lawrence Camp.	24/12/1916	25/12/1916
War Diary	Corps Reserve St Lawrence Camp. G.11.C.	26/12/1916	31/12/1916
Heading	10th North Fus: Jany-Oct 1917		
Miscellaneous	General Edmonds. Index To Correspondence File.		
War Diary	A Position Left Sector HQ. Tuilleries.	01/01/1917	04/01/1917
War Diary	C Position Inf Barracks	05/01/1917	08/01/1917
War Diary	A Position Left Sector	08/01/1917	12/01/1917
War Diary	D Position Inf. Barracks	12/01/1917	16/01/1917
War Diary	Lawrence Camp.	17/01/1917	24/01/1917
War Diary	St Lawrence Camp.	24/01/1917	24/01/1917
War Diary	B Battn Right Sector	24/01/1917	28/01/1917
War Diary	C Position Bund.	29/01/1917	31/01/1917
Miscellaneous	10th Battalion Northumberland Fusiliers Training Programme. 17th To 24th January, 1917	17/01/1917	17/01/1917
War Diary	C Position Bund.	01/02/1917	01/02/1917
War Diary	B Position Rl. Sector.	02/02/1917	05/02/1917
War Diary	D Position Bund.	05/02/1917	09/02/1917
War Diary	St Lawrence Camp.	10/02/1917	17/02/1917
War Diary	'B' Pos. Left Sector	18/02/1917	22/02/1917
War Diary	C Position Left Sector. Inf. Barr.	22/02/1917	26/02/1917
War Diary	G Camp	27/02/1917	27/02/1917
War Diary	Houtkerque.	28/02/1917	28/02/1917
Operation(al) Order(s)	Battalion Operation Order No. 100		
Operation(al) Order(s)	10th Battalion Northumberland Fusiliers Operation Order No. 101		
Operation(al) Order(s)	10th Battalion Northumberland Fusiliers. Operation Order No. 102		
Operation(al) Order(s)	10th Battalion Northumberland Fusiliers. Operation Order No. 103	16/02/1917	16/02/1917
Operation(al) Order(s)	10th Battalion The Northumberland Fusiliers. Operation Order No. 103	21/02/1917	21/02/1917
Operation(al) Order(s)	10th Battalion The Northumberland Fusiliers. Operation Order No. 105	24/02/1917	24/02/1917
Operation(al) Order(s)	10th Battalion Northumberland Fusiliers. Operation Order No. 106		
War Diary	Houtkerque. Millain.	01/03/1917	01/03/1917
War Diary	Millain	02/03/1917	18/03/1917
War Diary	Herzeele	19/03/1917	19/03/1917
War Diary	Y Camp.	20/03/1917	20/03/1917

Type	Description	Date From	Date To
War Diary	St Janter Brigade.	21/03/1917	21/03/1917
War Diary	'D' Camp.	22/03/1917	23/03/1917
War Diary	A.30.A. Sheet. 28 N.W.	23/03/1917	28/03/1917
War Diary	Hqrs L Defences Machine-Gun Farm	29/03/1917	31/03/1917
War Diary	L Lines. Elverdinghe Defences. H.Q. M-G Farm.	01/04/1917	04/04/1917
War Diary	D Camp A.30.D.	05/04/1917	05/04/1917
War Diary	Bullezeele	05/04/1917	13/04/1917
War Diary	St Lawrence Camp G.11.C.	13/04/1917	14/04/1917
War Diary	Hooge Sector. Left Batten (Left-Sub-Sector)	15/04/1917	17/04/1917
War Diary	Left Battn Hooge Sector.	18/04/1917	23/04/1917
War Diary	Support Battn. Hooge Sector	24/04/1917	30/04/1917
Operation(al) Order(s)	10th Battalion Northumberland Fusiliers Operation Order No. 110. App A.	04/04/1917	04/04/1917
Operation(al) Order(s)	10th Battalion Northumberland Fusiliers Operation Order No. 112. App "B".	04/04/1917	04/04/1917
Operation(al) Order(s)	10th Battalion Northumberland Fusiliers Operation Order. App. C.	10/04/1917	10/04/1917
Operation(al) Order(s)	10th Battalion Northumberland Fusiliers. Continuation Of Operation Order No. 112. App D.	12/04/1917	12/04/1917
Operation(al) Order(s)	10th Battalion Northumberland Fusiliers Operation Order No. 113. App E.	14/04/1917	14/04/1917
Operation(al) Order(s) Miscellaneous	Operation Order No. 114		
Miscellaneous	10th Battalion Northlds. Fusiliers Warning Order. App. E	16/04/1917	16/04/1917
Miscellaneous	10th Battalion Northumberland Fusiliers.		
Miscellaneous	App G.	18/04/1917	18/04/1917
Operation(al) Order(s)	Battalion Operation Order No. 116. Appendix H.		
Miscellaneous Diagram etc	To. 68th Inf. Brigade Hqrs. Report On Patrol. App I.	23/04/1917	23/04/1917
Operation(al) Order(s)	10th Battn Northd. Fusiliers Operation Order No. 117 App. J.	22/04/1917	22/04/1917
Operation(al) Order(s)	10th Battalion Northumberland Fusiliers Operation Order No. 118. App K.	24/04/1917	24/04/1917
Operation(al) Order(s)	10th Battalion Northumberland Fusiliers Operation Order No. 119. App L.	27/04/1917	27/04/1917
Operation(al) Order(s)	Battalion Operation Order. No. 120. App.17	30/04/1917	30/04/1917
War Diary	Steenvorde Training Area.	01/05/1917	10/05/1917
War Diary	Right Battn Hill 60 Sector	11/05/1917	18/05/1917
War Diary	Vancouver Camp.	19/05/1917	30/05/1917
War Diary	Rt. Sub Sect. Hill 60	31/05/1917	03/06/1917
War Diary	Right Battn Hill. 60	03/06/1917	06/06/1917
War Diary	'P' Camp.	06/06/1917	07/06/1917
War Diary	Reserve To 23rd Div.	08/06/1917	10/06/1917
War Diary	P Camp	11/06/1917	12/06/1917
War Diary	Dickebusch.	12/06/1917	21/06/1917
War Diary	Thieushouk	22/06/1917	30/06/1917
Operation(al) Order(s)	Battalion Operation Order No. 130. App A	06/06/1917	06/06/1917
Miscellaneous	Report On Operation From 6th To The 9th June. 1917. App "B"	09/06/1917	09/06/1917
Operation(al) Order(s)	Battalion Operation Order No. 131. App "C"	12/06/1917	12/06/1917
Operation(al) Order(s)	Battalion Operation Order No. 132. App D	20/06/1917	20/06/1917
Operation(al) Order(s)	Preliminary Battalion Operation Order No. 133. App E	28/06/1917	28/06/1917
Operation(al) Order(s)	Battalion Operation Order No. 133	29/06/1917	29/06/1917
War Diary	Micmac Camp.	01/07/1917	05/07/1917
War Diary	Mount Sorrel Sector.	06/07/1917	13/07/1917

Type	Description	From	To
War Diary	Micmac Camp.	14/07/1917	21/07/1917
War Diary	Thieushoek	22/07/1917	31/07/1917
Operation(al) Order(s)	Battalion Operation Order No. 134. App. A.	04/07/1917	04/07/1917
Operation(al) Order(s)	Operation Order No. 135. App. B.	08/07/1917	08/07/1917
Operation(al) Order(s)	Battalion Operation Order No. 136. App. C.		
Operation(al) Order(s)	10th Battalion Northumberland Fusiliers. Operation Order No. 137. App. D.	20/07/1917	20/07/1917
Operation(al) Order(s)	Battalion Operation Order No. 138. App E.		
War Diary	Setques.	01/08/1917	08/08/1917
War Diary	Serques	09/08/1917	24/08/1917
War Diary	Ottawa Camp.	25/08/1917	29/08/1917
War Diary	Dickebusch.	30/08/1917	31/08/1917
Operation(al) Order(s)	Battalion Operation Order.139	09/08/1917	09/08/1917
Operation(al) Order(s)	Battalion Operation Order No. 140	23/08/1917	23/08/1917
Heading	War Diary Of 10th (S) Battalion, Northumberland Fusiliers. From. Sept. 1st 1917. To. Sept. 30th 1917. Vol 25		
War Diary	Dickebusch	01/09/1917	01/09/1917
War Diary	Palace Camp.	02/09/1917	02/09/1917
War Diary	Steenvoorde	03/09/1917	04/09/1917
War Diary	Noordpene Area.	05/09/1917	13/09/1917
War Diary	Steenvoorde.	14/09/1917	14/09/1917
War Diary	Ottawa Camp.	15/09/1917	16/09/1917
War Diary	Dickebusch.	17/09/1917	18/09/1917
War Diary	Bedford House.	19/09/1917	20/09/1917
War Diary	Torr Top Tunnels.	21/09/1917	21/09/1917
War Diary	Bedford House.	22/09/1917	22/09/1917
War Diary	Sanctuary Wood	23/09/1917	23/09/1917
War Diary	Dickebusch.	24/09/1917	25/09/1917
War Diary	Kenora Camp.	26/09/1917	28/09/1917
War Diary	Brook Camp.	29/09/1917	30/09/1917
Miscellaneous	Battalion Operation Order. No. App. A	02/09/1917	02/09/1917
Miscellaneous	Operation Order. App B	02/09/1917	02/09/1917
Operation(al) Order(s)	Battalion Operation Order No. 143. App C.	04/09/1917	04/09/1917
Operation(al) Order(s)	Battalion Operation Order. No. 145. App. D	12/09/1917	12/09/1917
Operation(al) Order(s)	Battalion Operation Orders. No. 146. App. E	13/09/1917	13/09/1917
Operation(al) Order(s)	Battalion Operation Orders No, 147. App. F	15/09/1917	15/09/1917
Operation(al) Order(s)	Battalion Operation Orders No. 148. App. G	18/09/1917	18/09/1917
Miscellaneous	Operation Order. App. H.	21/09/1917	21/09/1917
Operation(al) Order(s)	Battalion Operation Orders. No. 149. App I	24/09/1917	24/09/1917
Operation(al) Order(s)	Battalion Operation Orders. No. 150. App J	27/09/1917	27/09/1917
Operation(al) Order(s)	Battalion Operation Orders No. 151. App. K.	29/09/1917	29/09/1917
War Diary	Brook Camp.	01/10/1917	01/10/1917
War Diary	Berthen Area.	02/10/1917	02/10/1917
War Diary	Thieushook Area.	03/10/1917	08/10/1917
War Diary	Brook Camp.	09/10/1917	09/10/1917
War Diary	Scottish Wood.	10/10/1917	13/10/1917
War Diary	Railway Dugouts.	14/10/1917	22/10/1917
War Diary	Longuenesse	23/10/1917	31/10/1917
Operation(al) Order(s)	Battalion Operation Order. No. 152. App. A.	01/10/1917	01/10/1917
Operation(al) Order(s)	Battalion Operation Order. No. 152. App. B.	01/10/1917	01/10/1917
Operation(al) Order(s)	Battalion Operation Order No. 153. App. C	07/10/1917	07/10/1917
Operation(al) Order(s)	Operation Order No. 153. App. D.	12/10/1917	12/10/1917
Miscellaneous	A Form. Messages And Signals.		
Operation(al) Order(s)	Operation Order No. 1. App. F.	18/10/1917	18/10/1917
Operation(al) Order(s)	Battalion Operation Order. No. 156. App. G.		

| Miscellaneous | Operation Order App. H | 20/10/1917 | 20/10/1917 |
| Operation(al) Order(s) | Operation Order No. 52 App. I. | 21/10/1917 | 21/10/1917 |

WO95/2182/3

10 Bn N'berland Fus

Aug 1915 - Oct 1917

23RD DIVISION
68TH INFY BDE

10TH BN NORTH'D FUS.
AUG 1915-FEB 1919

1917 OCT

To ITALY

68/23

10th North'n Fus:

Jany — Dec 1916

Index.........................

app. August

SUBJECT.

German
Accounts
Battle of
Le Cateau

$\frac{131}{7198}$

68/23 K.W."

10² Northumbd. Ave.

Vol I

Aug' Sep' 15
Feb '19

1-e

5/10/15

Army Form C. 2118.

WAR DIARY
or 10 North Staffs
INTELLIGENCE SUMMARY.

(Erase heading not required.)

Instructions regarding War Diaries and Intelligence Summaries are contained in F. S. Regs., Part II. and the Staff Manual respectively. Title pages will be prepared in manuscript.

Place	Date 1915	Hour	Summary of Events and Information	Remarks and references to Appendices
Brocton	Aug 25	4.50pm	A & B Coys, C.O. & Adjutant left.	S.9
		5.47pm	C & D Coys, 2ⁿᵈ in Command & M.G. Third left.	
Folkestone	Aug 26	8.30pm	A & B Cy, C.O & Adjutant arrived left.	S.9
		9.30pm	C & D Coy, 2ⁿᵈ in Command & M.G. Third left.	
Boulogne	Aug 26	10.30pm	A & B Coys C.O & Adjutant arrived marched into Rest Camp at Ostrohove.	S.9
		12.0 a.m.	C & D — Ditto Command & M.G. Officer at the Station	
Pointe Souper Aug 26 Station		10.20pm	The Battalion left and met the Transport Section & M.G. Section who had proceeded via Souttes to Harres	S.9
Harres			On the 24ᵗʰ August. Whole Battalion complete arrived at Ordnance at 2.0pm when the C.O. was informed that Battalion lines obtain at bottom.	

WARY DIARY
or
INTELLIGENCE SUMMARY.

Army Form C. 2118.

Place	Date	Hour	Summary of Events and Information	Remarks and references to Appendices
Watten	Aug 26	2:30 p.m	Arrived Watten at 2:30pm. Returned and marched into billets at Ganspette. Length of billets 2 miles. Time of arrival 3.30pm. Billets arranged by Staff Captain 6th Corps.	87.
Ganspette	Aug 27	9.0a - 1.0pm	Inspection of feet. Equipment. ammunition - rifles - billets.	87.
"	28th		In billets.	87.
"	29th			87.
"	30th		Billets	87.
"	31st			87.
"	Sept 1st	7.0am to 1.15pm	Divisional Service. Med Off 7.0am. buried Sergeo 8.30am. Left 11.30am & returned by Walten, reaching billets 1.15pm. Nom. Roll at	87

Army Form C. 2118.

WAR DIARY
or
INTELLIGENCE SUMMARY.
(Erase heading not required.)

Instructions regarding War Diaries and Intelligence Summaries are contained in F. S. Regs., Part II. and the Staff Manual respectively. Title pages will be prepared in manuscript.

Place	Date	Hour	Summary of Events and Information	Remarks and references to Appendices
Guarbette	Sept 2		Billets - Raining -	S.J.
"	Sept 3		Billets - Raining - Lecture by S.O.C. to Senior Officers of Battn	S.J.
"	Sept 4		In Billets	S.J.
"	" 5		In Billets	S.J.
"	6th	6.30pm	Batt. left Guarbette and reached Hazebrouck at 3.30pm - Route via Billets in Hospice (le Nouvel) - Very tiring march - a lot of fuelling	
"			Out - all rejoined in evening.	S.J.
Hazebrouck	7th	9.30am	Batt. left Hazebrouck and marched into Billets South of Borthend - Very hot march - a lot of fuelling out - all rejoined in evening ½ aft 1. (Cpl Evans).	S.J.
S. Borthend	8th	4.15pm	Inspection by Major General Pulteney, Cmg. 3rd Army Corps -	S.J.

2353 Wt. W2544/1454 700,000 5/15 D. D. & L. A.D.S.S./Forms/C. 2118.

WAR DIARY or INTELLIGENCE SUMMARY

Army Form C. 2118.

Place	Date	Hour	Summary of Events and Information	Remarks and references to Appendices
Spoilbank	Sept 9th	3:0 pm	Companies marched to Estaires independently and from there to Laventie into trenches - A & B Coys with 11th (S) Batt.n K.R.R.C. (Vice August Regt.) (? R. Hosp?) C & D Coys with 10th (S) Batt.n R.B. Rations were very late owing to a mix up, and companies did not get into the trenches until 10:30 pm. One casualty, wounded in knee.	S1.
Trenches	10th		At work on Doorn Trench etc. Relieved at 2:15 pm by 11 K.R.R. Enemy shelled 'B' Battery into shelters and Laventie - without effect.	S1.
Laventie	11th		+ returned in morning. 100 men from A, B & C Coys formed a digging party in billets. D Coy joined the 11th R.B. in the fg. with the 10th K.R.R.C. - 11 K.R.R. trenches & attd to 10th R.B. trenches. Relieved A & B went into 11 K.R.R. trenches. 2 casualties, wounded ankle & by tic.	S1.
Trenches	12th		Work during day on Doorn Trench - Relieved in evening by 11 K.R.R. and returned to billets - Enemy active in afternoon -	
Laventie	13th		Inspection etc. Absent with trenches with 10th K.R.R.C. Lieut Douglas Pennant, Capt A.F. Scott, 2 2nd Lts sick + forearm.	

Cy with 11th R.B.

WAR DIARY
or
INTELLIGENCE SUMMARY.

(Erase heading not required.)

Army Form C. 2118.

Place	Date	Hour	Summary of Events and Information	Remarks and references to Appendices
Trenches	Sept 14th		Trenches. One wounded slightly (at duty) - Relieved by 11th N.F.	87.
Lambre	15th		Billets. Battalion marched out at 6.30 pm by Companies and bivouaced in a field N of River Lys about 1½ miles N.E. of ESTAIRES.	87.
Aire	16th		Inspection of kit etc.	87.
"	17th		Battalion marched at 4.20 am into billets at Jesus Farm, vicinity of 1st A.D. Stephendres, 27th Division, arrived at 6.0 am	87.
Jesus Farm	18th		Billets.	
"	19th		Billets. Divine Service 11.0am JESUS FARM. Major Dodd, Major Ashton, Capt Norfolk went to ARRET to inspect trenches now occupied by 70th Inf Bde.	87.
"	20th		Billets. C Coy working party. Capt Llewellyn, R.A. & 2/Lt. Ellis inspected trenches	87.
"	21st		" Capt Foster, Lincoln, M.G. Officer, & 2 in command inspected trenches	87.
"	22		" A & B Coys each found working parties - Ammunition Ambulance	87.

Army Form C. 2118.

WAR DIARY
or
INTELLIGENCE SUMMARY.
(Erase heading not required.)

Instructions regarding War Diaries and Intelligence Summaries are contained in F. S. Regs., Part II. and the Staff Manual respectively. Title pages will be prepared in manuscript.

Place	Date Sept	Hour	Summary of Events and Information	Remarks and references to Appendices
Donnekin	23rd		Billets – C.O.D working parties	87
"	24th		" Entrenchment trained.	87
"	25th		A.T.B working parties – British & French attached.	87
"	26th		Left Jesus Farm at 3.0 pm – arrived in billets in ESTAIRES	87
		5.15pm	– attached to 20th Division – 2,600 prisoners taken by the French – Our advance in Champagne limited to 1600 yds by the French.	
ESTAIRES	27th		Remained in reserve all day – Left ESTAIRES at 6.0pm – arrived in billets at JESUS FARM at 8.10 pm.	87
JESUS FARM	28th		Left billets at 3.0 PM arrived in ESTAIRES at 6.0 PM	87
ESTAIRES	29th		Billets in ESTAIRES.	87
"	30th		Billets. Sent 80 men to 173rd Tunnelling Coy R.E.	87
"	Oct 1st		Orders to move tomorrow – Wounded, O.R. 1 (with Tunnelling Party)	87

121/7595.

2e

23rd Division

16th Northumberland Fus:
Vol 2
Oct 15

Q

WAR DIARY or INTELLIGENCE SUMMARY

Army Form C. 2118.

10th North Fusiliers   October 1915

Place	Date	Hour	Summary of Events and Information	Remarks and references to Appendices
ESTAIRES	Oct 2nd	9.0am	Left ESTAIRES at 9.0 am - arrived JESUS FARM at 11.0 am. Left JESUS FARM at 5.0 pm & relieved 11th WEST YORKS (69th Bde) Right Sector Trenches. A.B, D Coys firing trench. T.52, 53 & 54 - Afternoon thickening - Right Sector Trenches S.S. 54 - Relief completed 10.45 pm. "C" Coy in Support trench.	87.
Firing Trenches	3rd		Improving Trenches & setting down - Trenches very muddy. Prepared to thickening. Parados require much strengthening. Were nearly a great deal of repairing. Quiet day. Verrey Light (enemy) at night. S.S. 54 shelled -	87
"	4th		3 shots dropped from aeroplane near HQ (Belmond). T. 52 shelled. wounded one man. Our supply B Coy hit. Quiet night. Casualties wounded O.R. 2.	87.
"	5th		Pte R.C. Foster died from wounds 2.45 am - 29th Field Ambulance - Pte Knight wounded.	87.
"	6th		4th Battn relieved us - a good deal of M.G. fire during relief. We occupied Support trenches - (A & C Coys) - No stop in billets in RUE DELETTRES. "C" from barn	87

Army Form C. 2118.

WAR DIARY
or
INTELLIGENCE SUMMARY.

(Erase heading not required.)

Instructions regarding War Diaries and Intelligence Summaries are contained in F.S. Regs., Part II. and the Staff Manual respectively. Title pages will be prepared in manuscript.

Place	Date	Hour	Summary of Events and Information	Remarks and references to Appendices
Support Trenches & Hills	Oct 7th		Nothing unusual – working party 300 men – 7.0 p.m. Trouverey Avenue (WD)	87-
"	8th		"	87-
"	9th		Pte Malone (14747) wounded by sharpshooter	87-
"	10th		Working party of 50 men at bottom of Shaftesbury Avenue.	87
Front Trenches	12th		Relieved 9th N.F. in 'A' Position T.52, B.6y. T.52.B.6g. T.53.B.6y. T.54.C.6g. S.S.g. A5y	87
	13th		Day quiet – 4.15 am very heavy firing from battalion on right – no apparent reason – artillery fired 10 rds. Pte Hardy, Kilpatrick & Little killed	87-
"	14th		Work on Rampart Barras Ditch – quiet day	87-
"	15th		Nothing special – usual work	87-

WAR DIARY
or
INTELLIGENCE SUMMARY.

(Erase heading not required.)

Army Form C. 2118.

Instructions regarding War Diaries and Intelligence Summaries are contained in F.S. Regs., Part II. and the Staff Manual respectively. Title pages will be prepared in manuscript.

Place	Date	Hour	Summary of Events and Information	Remarks and references to Appendices
A trenches	Oct 16th		Quiet day – Relief by 11th N.Z. Relief commenced 6.15 pm – Completed 8.15 pm. Battalion moved in billets in 'D' portion at 9.40 pm. Battn. H.Q. or RUE DE BIEZ –	87.
D'Portion	17th		Battalion had Divisional Baths	87.
"	18th		Musketry – About Thurrey working parties	87.
"	19th		Musketry – About Thurrey working parties Div. baths in morning – Relieved 11th N.Z. in evening – Relief completed 8.6 pm –	87.
"	20th		Amalgamated with 1st Nmzd [Reinforcements] formed two companies battalions as follows :– D'Portion	87.

A trenches Batt. H.Qrs. 10th N.Z.
52
53
54
S. 54

B. Coy 10th N.Z.
A Coy 1st S.F.
Aux 1st S.F.
D Coy 10th N.Z.
C Coy 1st S.F.

D Portion Batt. H.Qrs. 1st S.F.
A } 3 coy
C } 3 coy
B } 3 coy
D } 3 coy

1st S.F.
10th N.Z.
1st S.F.

Army Form C. 2118.

WAR DIARY
or
INTELLIGENCE SUMMARY.
(Erase heading not required.)

Instructions regarding War Diaries and Intelligence Summaries are contained in F. S. Regs., Part II. and the Staff Manual respectively. Title pages will be prepared in manuscript.

Place	Date	Hour	Summary of Events and Information	Remarks and references to Appendices
A Tunnels	Oct 21st		Quiet day – Enemy fired about 10 HE shells into 54 & S9. Not many – On D102 replied with 5 shells (shrapnel) – 4 hit German parapet.	87.
"	22nd		Enemy fired 16 shells into parapet of 52 – 3 hit parapet + 2 phonoes. Enemy very noisy at 'Stand To' at 5.0pm. Shooting – Strullen, Pte Southwick & Newsom killed – Pte Wardle wounded	87
"	23rd		Enemy bombarded 52 trench for not an hour in the morning, mostly HE – Shooting crater – shells firing into No Mans Land. Parapet, phonoes, Wok beam, Joyd stand in front of listed batt 18"Whz B'ly Cookhouse destroyed – Pte Cockman killed, Pte Dawson wounded – very accurate but not effective – our artillery replied with shrapnel.	87
"	24th M.		Very quiet all day except – Two officers patrols tried to work for from Pt C (attached appendix) went out - returning that morning from 6.15pm – 7.15pm. from 10.0pm – 12.0 pm – no result	87

WAR DIARY
or
INTELLIGENCE SUMMARY.

Army Form C. 2118.

Place	Date	Hour	Summary of Events and Information	Remarks and references to Appendices
'A' Trenches	Oct 28th	6.0pm	Relieved by 11th N.Z. - Relief completed by 7.30pm - Returned to 'C' Ponton A + C in support trenches, B + D in billets - Platemough + moving	S.I.
'C' Ponton	Oct 28th		Nothing particular. B + D Coys now refitted	S.I.
	Oct 29th			
	Oct 29th			
'C' Ponton	Oct 29th	6.0pm	Relieved 11th N.Z. but into 'A' Ponton - A Coy S2, C Coy S3, B Coy S4, A Coy S.S4	S.I.
'A' Trenches	Oct 30th		Enemy fired 70 shells into S1, S3, Jocks Joy + Nott + HQ's between 11.0am at 12.30pm - Nothing - No guns retaliated.	S.I.
'A' Trenches	Oct 31st		Quiet all day - Enemy opened heavy M.G. fire between 6.45pm + 7.45pm - No damage - Our M.G. retaliated at 8.0pm - fired 1288 rounds -	S.I.

Signed Sidney Jones Capt M.
Adjutant 10 North'd Fus.

3-e

23rd Division

10th N'thumb: Fus:
Vol: 3

12/11
1944

Nov 15.

10 A'mt [Fusiliers]

WAR DIARY
or
INTELLIGENCE SUMMARY.
(Erase heading not required.)

Army Form C. 2118.

Place	Date	Hour	Summary of Events and Information	Remarks and references to Appendices
A'Tunis	1915 Nov 1st		Transfers re-numbered as follows —	
			Old Numbers. New Numbers	
			52 1. 32.	
			53 1. 26/1.	
			54 1. 26/2.	
			S.S. 54 S.S. 1. 26/2.	
	Nov 2		Quiet day — wet	87.
			Very hot all day — relieved by 1st [Stafford] Foresters 6.0pm	
			went to JESUS FARM — attached to 24th Brigade — [Pritcham] killed	87
Jaros Farm	Nov 3		6th sent only, cond 24th Bde th Bde called — Place very muddy.	87
"	4th		Battalion had divisional baths — 220 working party	87
"	5th		Inspection by [Gen] [M...]	87.

Army Form C. 2118.

WAR DIARY
or
INTELLIGENCE SUMMARY.
(Erase heading not required.)

Instructions regarding War Diaries and Intelligence Summaries are contained in F. S. Regs., Part II. and the Staff Manual respectively. Title pages will be prepared in manuscript.

Place	Date 1915	Hour	Summary of Events and Information	Remarks and references to Appendices
Jesus Farm	Nov 6th		Working party – 220.	S.T.
"	" 7th		" 110	S.T.
"	" 8th		Battalion proceeded to D'Portion relieving 1st S. Forsters – Sprice asked. 220	S.T.
D Portion	9th		Apartment admitted to 71st 2nd Phantnham D portion –	S.T.
"	10th		Battalion relieved 11th North Forsters in 'A' Portion.	S.T.
A portion	11th		Quiet day	S.T.
"	12th		Enemy snipers active opposite Trench 52.	S.T.
"	13th		Quiet day – Relieved by 11th N. Fus. and proceeded to C Portion.	C.T.

Army Form C. 2118.

WAR DIARY
or
INTELLIGENCE SUMMARY.

(Erase heading not required.)

10th November

Place	Date	Hour	Summary of Events and Information	Remarks and references to Appendices
1915	Nov 14			
C Parton	Nov 14 to Nov 17		working parties daily	S.1.
	Nov 17		Relieved by 1st Sherwood Foresters & proceeded to JESUS FARM for 8 days REST.	S.1.
JESUS FARM	18th		Cleaning & refitting	S.1.
"	19th			
"	20th		Inspection by G.O.C. 68th Bde.	S.1.
"	21st			
"	6 h		} In rest.	
"	24th			S.1.
"	24th		Relieved 9th York Regt in A position LEFT SECTOR Trenches 57. 58. 59. 60 & 61. Distribution. A Cy 57 + ½ 58, B Cy ½ 58 + 59, C Cy 60, D Cy 61 } Salient	S.1.

Army Form C. 2118.

WAR DIARY
or
INTELLIGENCE SUMMARY.

(Erase heading not required.)

Place	Date 1915.	Hour	Summary of Events and Information	Remarks and references to Appendices
LEFT SECTOR A. Position	Nov 25th		LEFT SECTOR Quiet day.	SA.
"	Nov 26th		Pte E. Danly. A Coy., wounded. Some shelling of Batt HQrs.	SA.
"	27th		Pte F. Robson C Coy - wounded	SA.
"	28th		Pte A. Sonans D Coy - killed - position - RUE MARLE. Relieved by 11th N.F. and proceeded to D	SA.
D Position	29th		} Daily working parties.	SA.
"	30th			SA.
"	Dec 1st		Relieved 11th N.F. in A. Position. Same disposition as on Nov 24th.	SA.
"	Dec 2nd		Some shelling. L/Cpl J.R Richardson. D Coy } killed. Pte A.J. Hanson. C Coy }	SA.
"	Dec 4th		Quiet	SA.
"	Dec 5th		Corporal M. Pringle A Coy, wounded.	SA.

Sydney Green Capt
Adjutant 10th Northumb

10th Northumbd: Fus:
Vol: 4

1/2/
7910

23rd R's

Paid night of 31st Dec/1 Jan

WAR DIARY
or
INTELLIGENCE SUMMARY.
(Erase heading not required.)

10th North'd Fus

Place	Date	Hour	Summary of Events and Information	Remarks and references to Appendices
A Position	1915 Sept 7th		LEFT SECTOR. Relieved by 11th N. Fus and proceeded to C position (Bde) Keeps in RUE MARLE, A Cy in Reserve Trench, D Cy in CHAPELLE D'ARMENTIERES	RUE MARLE S.7. CHAPELLE D'ARMENTIERES S.7.
C Position	"8th"		Small working parties.	
"	"9th"		RUE MARLE shelled for an hour - Pte M.N. Colman, B Cy, killed. Some shelling of CHAPELLE D'ARMENTIERES & SANDBAG CORNER. Ptes J. Thompson, C Cy, J.W. Ryan & A Cy. slightly wounded (at duty)	S.7. SANDBAG S.7.
"	"10th"		Relieved 11th N.Fus in A Position.	

WAR DIARY or INTELLIGENCE SUMMARY

Army Form C. 2118.

Place	Date	Hour	Summary of Events and Information	Remarks and references to Appendices
A Fonton	1915 Dec 1st		LEFT SECTOR Artillery cut wire in front of 1.26/5 & 1.20/1 - von MG fired on it during the night.	S1.
"	Dec 2nd		Pte R.W. Hodgson D.Cy (2nd in C's Osborn) wounded in DOG LEG ROAD	S1.
"	Dec 3rd		Redistribution of front line - 3 Coy 2 Coy & 2 platoons in front line 1 Coy & 1 platoon in BOIS GRENIER line. as follows - A Coy (2 platoons) 1.26/5 & ½ 1.20/1 B Coy. ½ 1.20/1, ½ 1.20/2 & ½ 1.21/2 [SALIENT]. D Coy & A Coy (1 platoon) ½ 1.21/1 & 1.21/2 BOIS GRENIER line. C. Coy & A Coy (1 platoon)	S1.
"	14th		Relieved by 1st Sherwood Foresters and proceeded to RUE DORMOIRE (Divl. Reserve) - arrived 9.0 pm. Capt O.J. Clifton 103rd Wdh R.F.A attempt to prise in SALIENT.	S1.

WAR DIARY
or
INTELLIGENCE SUMMARY.

(Erase heading not required.)

Place	Date	Hour	Summary of Events and Information	Remarks and references to Appendices
RUE DORMOIRE	Dec 15th 1915		Presentation of V.C. to Pte Kenny, 13th D.L.I. by Lt General Sir W. Pulteney, KCB, DSO, G.O.C. 3rd Corps — 4 Officers + 32 men of the battalion under the Adjutant attended.	87.
"	Dec 16th to Dec 21st		Refitting, Cleaning — Bomb practice, Musketry & Bayonet practice — Small working parts of 50 daily.	87.
	Dec 22		Relieved 10th WEST RIDING REGT in D[ranoutre]. RIGHT SECTOR H.Q. & M.G. H.11.C.6.5. A H.11.C.2.6. C A.17.D.7.2. B H.16.C.6.7. D H.11.D.0.4. Very heavy rain.	87.
D'ranoutre Right Sector	23.			87.
"	to Jan 9.		Working party of 100 to keep 11th N.Z. in front line trenches A front line	87.

WAR DIARY
or
INTELLIGENCE SUMMARY.
(Erase heading not required.)

Place	Date 1915	Hour	Summary of Events and Information	Remarks and references to Appendices
Mess D Position Ruptshute	Dec 25		Nothing special –	87
"	Dec 26		Relieved 11th N. Fus in B Position Ruptshute – 2½ h.p. in Front Line 1½ h.p. – BOIS GRENIER	87
"	27th		Nothing special –	87
"	28th		Raiding Party under Capt. Ruffek remained in billets practising for Raid on Dec 29/n 15	87
"	29th			87
"	30th		Relieved by 11th N. F. 2's + proceeded to B Position	87

WAR DIARY
or
INTELLIGENCE SUMMARY.

(Erase heading not required.)

Place	Date	Hour	Summary of Events and Information	Remarks and references to Appendices
C Portion Ripont Sector	1915 Dec 31		Report of Minor Enterprise carried out by the Battalion on the night of Dec 31st 1915 / Jan 1st 1916.	
"	1916 Jan 1st		**Raid on German Trenches**	
			The men were selected by Capt. A.W. Norfolk chiefly from his own company and were all billeted together.	
			The attack was practised by day & night on ground which resembled the actual ground as much as possible.	
			Patrols were sent out from our front line on 28th, 29th & 30th Dec: & not under officers, the men of the patrol being taken from the raiding party so as to accustom them to the lie of the ground. The reports received from the patrols proved that the enemy's listening post in front of I.26.6.4.2 was occupied on each occasion the patrol went out.	

WAR DIARY
or
INTELLIGENCE SUMMARY.

(Erase heading not required.)

Instructions regarding War Diaries and Intelligence Summaries are contained in F. S. Regs., Part II. and the Staff Manual respectively. Title pages will be prepared in manuscript.

Army Form C. 2118.

Place	Date	Hour	Summary of Events and Information	Remarks and references to Appendices
			On the night 31/1 the party left their billets at 10.30 P.M. and proceeded up to the front line. All bridges, blocking frames etc. having been carried up some time previous to this and placed in a position of readiness in our line.	
			I & my Adjutant left our billets at 6.30 P.M. to ascertain that all the wires to the various batteries & Machine Guns were in proper order, & that the searchlights & other details were in their proper places. There were two F.O. Officers, R.A. & signaller operators with me at point I.26.6.A.H.2. & the battalion signallers were close by me to work the M.G., Brigade, & Battalion Headquarters lines.	
			Two lines of our wires had been previously cut by the 11th North'd Fusiliers at point of exit & entry & this battalion assisted	

WAR DIARY
or
INTELLIGENCE SUMMARY.

(Erase heading not required.)

Instructions regarding War Diaries and Intelligence Summaries are contained in F.S. Regs., Part II. and the Staff Manual respectively. Title pages will be prepared in manuscript.

Place	Date	Hour	Summary of Events and Information	Remarks and references to Appendices
			me by finding the trench party of one officer & 20 men. At 12.45 a.m. 1st Jany the covering party under Lieut. Reid left our trenches & took up their allotted position at point I.26.c.8.3½ to I.26.c.5½.2, & at 12.25 a.m. the assaulting party under Lieut. Allan began to leave our trenches. There was some difficulty experienced in getting the bridges & blocking obstacles over the parapets as they were rather heavy. This party was clear of our wire & ready in position to move at 12.50 a.m. Lieut Allan the then cutters, followed by the bridging & remainder of the assaulting party, then moved off; the ground was covered with coarse grass and crossing in silence was difficult, but a strong wind was blowing in our favour.	

WAR DIARY
or
INTELLIGENCE SUMMARY.
(Erase heading not required.)

Place	Date	Hour	Summary of Events and Information	Remarks and references to Appendices
			Shortly after 1·0 A.M. Lieut Allan saw the German wire & their sentries could be heard talking & whistling. This party had not been detected up to this moment. The German wire was seen to have been well cut by our artillery & was lying on the ground, & no difficulty & no difficulty would have been experienced in getting through. Just at this time three shots were fired from the German listening post, & a very loud telephone buzzer was distinctly heard, whistles & gongs being sounded from the German lines. The Blocking party left our lines at 12.30 P.M. under Lieut Jacobs and had to move very slowly owing to the nature of the ground and it was when this party was in line with the German listening post that the Verey lights and	

Army Form C. 2118.

WAR DIARY
or
INTELLIGENCE SUMMARY.

(Erase heading not required.)

Instructions regarding War Diaries and Intelligence Summaries are contained in F. S. Regs., Part II. and the Staff Manual respectively. Title pages will be prepared in manuscript.

Place	Date	Hour	Summary of Events and Information	Remarks and references to Appendices
			whistles were sounded and it is evident that the Blocking party had what turn out or heard from the enemy's listening post; very heavy rifle + M.G. fire was then opened and a number of red + white lights were sent and about 10 to 12 minutes after, three searchlights played on No man's land and on our parapets and the enemy's artillery bombarded the support + back lines with H.E. + Shrapnel; this bombardment + rifle fire lasted some considerable time. At 1-20 A.M, knowing that our party could not possibly succeed in their enterprise I asked the V.O.O. to signal to the batteries not to fire as previously arranged at zero time. I reported what I had done to Brigade Headquarters. As the bombardment continued I asked for Retaliation in the hope of	

WAR DIARY
or
INTELLIGENCE SUMMARY.

Army Form C. 2118.
4 JAN. 1916

amongst the enemy's guns but this only seemed to increase their fire so I asked the F.O.O. to signal to our batteries to cease firing. This had the desired effect and all firing died down about 3.45 A.M.

The men of the raiding party came in slowly bringing the killed & wounded with them, at about 3.30 A.M. all were in except one man who was killed.

The dressing station placed in Dug out near the point of exit from our trenches proved to be of the greatest value.

The men composing the raiding party are greatly disappointed at the non-success of the operation, but luck was against them. The Artillery in cutting the enemy's wire had carried out their task very well, the wire having been seen lying in small

WAR DIARY
or
INTELLIGENCE SUMMARY.
(Erase heading not required.)

ORDERLY ROOM
- 4 JAN. 1916
Ba. Northumberland Fusiliers

Place	Date	Hour	Summary of Events and Information	Remarks and references to Appendices
			pieces on the ground & I received great assistance from the M.O. & attached to me. The 11th North'd Fusiliers assisted me by finding the trench party of 1 Officer, 2 N.C.O.'s & men. The Medical Officer who had only been doing duty with the battalion for one day previous to the raid helped in every possible way, going so far as to carry a wounded man on his back to relieve the stretcher bearers. I cannot speak too highly of his work. Capt Norfolk who was in command of the party was unfortunately wounded & therefore his report is not forthcoming. He carried out his orders perfectly. The casualties were as follows:- 1 Officer wounded (in both ankles)	Casualties Killed: Cpl Gordon D Cpl Antonio D Pte Willis D " Rolston D " Stout D " Dryden D " Red Maud Pte Irons A Pte Seeley A Pte McSmith D Wounded: Sergt Rutter Pte Tait Sgt Delaware L/C Falk L/C McRaven LI Col A. McRaven

WAR DIARY
or
INTELLIGENCE SUMMARY.
(Erase heading not required.)

Army Form C. 2118.

Place	Date	Hour	Summary of Events and Information	Remarks and references to Appendices
"C" Position	Jan 2		3 N.C.O's men killed.	Pte Clark D " Cullen D " Dring D " Horden A " McBrth D " Metcalf A " Johnson A " Keith D " Smith B " Lacey B Lt. H.W. Norfolk
			13 N.C.O's & men wounded (of whom three have died since)	
			One company whilst in billets had:—	
			2 N.C.O's men killed.	
			4 N.C.O's men wounded.	
			by H.E. shell. This company took no part in the raid. Capt H.W. Norfolk	87
"	Jan 3		Major Genl Babington C.B, C.M.G etc, cmd 23rd Divn interested & addressed the raiding party.	
"	to 4.		Relieved 11th N.F. in "B" position Left Sector. Pte Knight (S.5) 87. killed	
			Lieut Hunter (Actg) wounded.	

4 Jan 1916

Sydney S. ??? Capt
A???

10th Nathunch: Two:
Vol: 5

23

5 - e

Army Form C. 2118.

WAR DIARY
or
INTELLIGENCE SUMMARY.
(Erase heading not required.)

Instructions regarding War Diaries and Intelligence Summaries are contained in F. S. Regs., Part II. and the Staff Manual respectively. Title pages will be prepared in manuscript.

Place	Date	Hour	Summary of Events and Information	Remarks and references to Appendices
Laventie Left Sector	5th		Pte Chapp(Roland) wounded.	87.
"	6th		nil	87.
"	7th		Relieved by 1st Sherwood Foresters and proceeded to JESUS FARM	87
JESUS FARM	8th to 15th		⎱ nil ⎰	87.
"	15th		Relieved 9th 10th Rifts in D Portion. Left Sector - RUEMARLE. C.Cy - 3 Platoons in BOIS GRENIER line	87.
RUEMARLE	16th to 19th		⎱ nil - working parties ⎰	87
"	19th		Relieved 11th N.7 in A Portion Left Sector. Distribution. A Cy. 1.26.5 & 1.20.1 B Cy. 1.20.2 & 1.21.1 C Cy. 1.21.1 & 1.21.2 D Cy. BOISGRENIERline. 24461 Pte C. Harris, C. Cy wounded. (slight arm.)	87.

WAR DIARY or INTELLIGENCE SUMMARY

Army Form C. 2118.

Place	Date	Hour	Summary of Events and Information	Remarks and references to Appendices
A Portion Left Sector	1916 Feb 19th 20th		24440 Pte R. Richardson, C Coy, wounded	S.7.
	21st		NIL	S.7.
	22nd		Enemy bombarded the Salient for ½ hr at 3.0pm with Trench Mortars - wounded Lt. R.L. Smart. 14457 Pte J.J. Christop. B Coy. 16150 Pte R.D.G. Simpson B Coy.	S.7.
	23rd		wounded 19616 Pte J. Sains B Coy 12833 Pte T. Morton B Coy Relieved by 11th N.F and proceeded to C Portion Left Sector.	
			RUE MARLE - IA & B Coys in BOIS GRENIER Line. Head quarters were subjected to shelling, M.G. & rifle fire at 7.30pm on the DOG LEG road, so they were sniping at - no casualties.	S.7.
C Portion Left Sector	24th		Billets - Working Party.	

WAR DIARY or INTELLIGENCE SUMMARY

Army Form C. 2118.

Place	Date 1916	Hour	Summary of Events and Information	Remarks and references to Appendices
C Portion Left Sector	Jan 25th to 27th		Billets in RUE MARLE	87.
	27		Relieved 11th N.F. in A Portion Left Sector. Disposition: C Coy 1.26.5 & 1.20.1. BOIS GRENIER Line D Coy 1.20.2 & 1.21.1. B Coy A Coy 2.12.1.1 & 1.21.2. K Coy 15th R. Fusiliers attached to Bn. for instruction.	
			Heavy bombardment by enemy with H.E. Shrapnel & Trench Mortars on Salient A.11.1.10.9 & BOIS GRENIER - 500 shells - no casualties.	87.
A Portion Left Sector	28th		Heavy Bombardment of Peeling Lunas - 4.0am - 5.0am. 10.15am - 12.15pm. 3.0pm - 4.0pm. About 3000 shells - H.E. Shrapnel & Trench Mortars.	87.

WAR DIARY or INTELLIGENCE SUMMARY

Army Form C. 2118.

Place	Date 1916	Hour	Summary of Events and Information	Remarks and references to Appendices
A Sector Left Sector	Jan 28th		Casualties. 19531 Pte G. Collingwood, A Coy.	
			1699 Sgt T. Harvey, A Coy	
			19572 Pte Nicolas, A Coy	
			15625 Pte J. Rennell, A Coy	
			6207 " Crane, A Coy	
			19558 " Ritson, A Coy	
			14168 " McDonagh, D Coy	
			19513 L/C Houghton, D Coy	Wounded. S.1.
			15757 Pte B. Hayne, D Coy	
			19496 " Statler, D Coy	
			14863 " P. Brazier, D Coy	
			7746 " Jackson, D Coy	
			10392 L/C Stephenson, D Coy	
			19716 Pte Hoyle, C Coy (slightly wounded)	
			K Coy 15th Royal Scots left trenches and were replaced by M Coy 15th Royal Scots.	
	29th		Casualties. Capt R.A. Ellis (wounded) A Coy. Small Bombardment 1.20 pm to 2.0 pm	S.1.
			6040 Pte Smith, D Coy (wounded) by Trench Mortar. M Coy 15th R.S. relieved by K Coy 15th R.S.	

Army Form C. 2118.

WAR DIARY
or
INTELLIGENCE SUMMARY.
(Erase heading not required.)

Instructions regarding War Diaries and Intelligence Summaries are contained in F. S. Regs., Part II. and the Staff Manual respectively. Title pages will be prepared in manuscript.

Place	Date 1916	Hour	Summary of Events and Information	Remarks and references to Appendices
Ploegsteert Lift Sulo	Jan 30th		Quiet day. Bss/Cpl S.M. Hills.9. A Cy. killed. 9346 Cpl M. Lock.P. D Cy - wounded. Kern 15th R.S. replaced by M Cy 15th R.S.	S.7.
"	Jan 31.		Quiet day - 5106 Pte Wallace A Cy wounded 6221 " Anderson A Cy S (accdt) Battalion was relieved by 1st Sherwood Foresters and proceeded to Divisional Reserve at RUE DORMOIRE. M Cy 15th R.S. returned back to 11th N. Fus. 2i Coyt 11th Suffolks were attached to the Battalion for one day.	S.7.

Sydney Snew Capt.
Adj. 16th N.F.

WAR DIARY or INTELLIGENCE SUMMARY.

Army Form C. 2118.

ORDERLY ROOM
6 FEB 1916
1/1st (Ser.) Bn. Northumberland Fusiliers

Place	Date 1916	Hour	Summary of Events and Information	Remarks and references to Appendices
RUE DORMOIRE	Feb 1st		With reference to the account of the raid on the German Trenches on the morning of Jan 1st 1916, the Commanding Officer brought to notice the conduct of the following Officers, N.C.O.'s & men for exceptional work:—	
			Officers Capt A.M.W. Nottell. Lieut. J.L. Allen Lieut. F.L. Smart Lieut. P.R. Scott 2/Lt R.S. Hind 2/Lt J.L. Ward (Unkilled reconnaissance work). Lieut G. Murray Shaw RAMC, 70 Field Ambulance.	
			N.C.O's & men 10/6886 Sgt Mallen, W.N. 10/11545 Cpl Kirtley, L.G. 10/7011 L/Cpl McGuirk, G.W. 10/9822 " Scott, H. 10/9633 Pte Lavery, J. 10/1957 Pte Lockyard 10/13457 " Coulson, M. 10/9467 " Metcalfe, M.M.	
			During the enemy bombardment one H.E. Shell hit one of the company billets in RUE CHARLES, one man being killed & several wounded — Pte Metcalfe who was wounded in the leg & arm at the time, said nothing about his wounds. It was most auspicious as helping his wounded comrades — his Co. commander made one bring to notice his conduct & pluck on this occasion as Pte Metcalfe did not disclose his wounds until his comrades had been attended to. Sgt Mallen } brought in Cpl Notbell who was very Officer, forward & L/C McGuirk } under heavy rifle fire. The other men went (see) Pte Lockyard } out several times to bring in the killed & wounded Pte Lavery (wounded) } B.Stewart Lt Col Cmg 10th NF	

WAR DIARY or INTELLIGENCE SUMMARY

Army Form C. 2118.

10th North'n Fusiliers

Place	Date 1916	Hour	Summary of Events and Information	Remarks and references to Appendices
RUE DOUOVRE	Feb 1st		11th Suffolks left. Environs that my command of Brigade. Inniskillens march Serve of G.O.C. Brigade.	S.1.
"	2		Inspected by G.O.C. 23rd Division of Officers, N.C.O.'s, O.R.C. O's (incl. Corporals)	S.1.
"	3rd 4. 5.		Billets	S.1.
"	5th		R.A Band played in morning afternoon near Battalion's billets	S.1.
"	6th 7th		Billets	S.1.
"	8th		Relieved 8th Yorks in 'D' position Right Sector - ROLANDERIE FARM	S.1.
ROLANDERIE FARM	9th 10 11		Billets - working parties	S.1.
"	12		Relieved 11th N.F. in 'B' position Right Sector. Distribution as follows - A Coy + 2 platoons of B Coy N.F (C4) 1.32 + 1.26.1 B Coy ½ platoon of my R. 1.26.7 + 2 1.26.3 C Coy in pretive firm R + 2 1.21.3 + 2 1.6.4 Dly. Bois Grenier line	WOUNDED 6811 C/S Trust, Alfy. 196 96 Pte Snow, C.J.

ORDERLY ROOM
1 MAR 1916
10th (Serv) Bn. North'n Fusiliers

Army Form C. 2118.

WAR DIARY
or
INTELLIGENCE SUMMARY.
(Erase heading not required.)

Instructions regarding War Diaries and Intelligence Summaries are contained in F. S. Regs., Part II. and the Staff Manual respectively. Title pages will be prepared in manuscript.

Place	Date 1916	Hour	Summary of Events and Information	Remarks and references to Appendices
B POSITION RIGHT SECTOR	7/1/13	6.45a	Enemy's Artillery commenced shelling at B sector & continued all day steadily till 4.20 p.m.	K/
		2.30p	Enemy's fire increased in intensity & became very concentrated. Our 200 shells arrived here been fired during the day.	
		4.30p	Enemy's fire died down. Places shelled were 1.32, 1.26.1, 1.26.2, JOCK'S JOY, BATT. HR, S.S. 54, WATER FARM, MOAT FARM portions of the BOIS GRENIER line. At one time within 3 mins 40 shells burst at Jock's Joy (H² & this kep). Shelling consisted of 5.9", 4.2", 77's, motor aerial torpedoes. Casualties 6 wounded - material damage to trenches. Retaliation of the latter was supplied during the night. Our Artillery retaliated but see extent. It had no effect as well. To the North shelling. Our 18 pdrs were fired - but heavy from N.Horitzer fired at the holes made by the troth trench mortars. "C" Coy 2nd N.F. L.M. trenches in the evening and formed 11"N.F. at ROUANDERIE FARM.	WOUNDED 16210 L/CPL Dodds 9621 Pitman SC 9873 Shield Bay 6963 Smith Boy 1721 Bennin M² " Retson CC₂
				Lt J.T.Mehta 2 Lt E.Lawrence joined.

3353) Wt. W2544/1454 700,000 5/15 D. D. & L. A.D.S.S./Forms/C. 2118.

WAR DIARY
or
INTELLIGENCE SUMMARY.

Army Form C. 2118.

Place	Date 1916	Hour	Summary of Events and Information	Remarks and references to Appendices
B Postn RIGHT SECTOR	14th Sep		Very quiet all day - 14854 Pte T. Irwin "C" Coy killed 2/Lt J. Roarins, 2/Lt C.W. Martin + 93 O.R. (draft) joined.	8.7.
"	15th Sep		} Extremely quiet day.	8.7.
"	16th Sep			8.7.
"	17th Sep			8.7.
"	17th Sep		Relieved by 11th North Lancs. & proceeded to C' Anton. Right Sector.	8.7.
RUE DELETTRE	18th Sep to 20th Sep		} Wiring - daily working parties.	8.7.
"	21st Sep		Relieved by 10th Lincoln Regt & proceeded to JESUS FARM.	8.7.
JESUS FARM	22nd Sep		Refitting -	
	23rd Sep		Heard that Bgde had remain behind for a time in 1st Army Corps Rest.	8.7.

Army Form C. 2118.

WAR DIARY
or
INTELLIGENCE SUMMARY.
(Erase heading not required.)

Instructions regarding War Diaries and Intelligence Summaries are contained in F. S. Regs., Part II. (Sec.) and the Staff Manual respectively. Title pages will be prepared in manuscript.

Place	Date	Hour	Summary of Events and Information	Remarks and references to Appendices
JESUS PORT JELANI			NIL.	81.
JESUS PORT JELANI	24th	10.0am	Left for BAC ST MAUR - arrived 12.0 noon - Entrained Billets pm 23rd N.7 (4th Tyneside Scottish)	81.
BAC ST MAUR	26/26	10.0am	Left for MORBECQUE - arrived at 5.10pm - 17 mile march - no hitch. No hitch between property arrived - Transport Billets were occupied by Ordnance. Pub billets had to be obtained - all complete by 9.0pm	81.
MORBECQUE	27 28th		Billets.	81.
MORBECQUE	29th	6.0am	Transport left for COLONNE RICQUART - arrived at MARNES LES MINES about 3.0pm.	81.
		2.0pm	Battalion left by train from STEENBECQUE Station at 1 o'clock for COLONNE RICQUART at 3.30 P.M.- Detrained at marched to billets in MARNES LES MINES at 4.30pm	81.

Lindsay Young Capt
Adjutant 10th North'd Fus

A.D.S.S./Forms/C. 2118.

Army Form C. 2118.

WAR DIARY
or
INTELLIGENCE SUMMARY.

(Erase heading not required.)

Instructions regarding War Diaries and Intelligence Summaries are contained in F. S. Regs., Part II. and the Staff Manual respectively. Title pages will be prepared in manuscript.

Place	Date 1916	Hour	Summary of Events and Information	Remarks and references to Appendices
MARNES LES MINES	March 1st		Nills	81.
"	2nd	12.14pm	Battalion inspected by Lt Gen Sir H. Wilson KCB, Comd IV Corps	81.
"	3rd to 7th		} Nills	83.
"	8th	6.30am	Fire started in no 3 platoon billet - reported from 7.0p - 12.0 mn started by overturned candle lighting the straw in the room. Left MARNES LES MINES and Marched via MOUDAIN, REBREUVE, FRESNICOURT to billets in VERDREL. arrived 12.30pm. Harambe.	81.
VERDREL	9th		NIL	81.
	10th		Billets.	9W
	11th		Billets.	9W
	12th		Billets. Ch Ronan left. Ravier jones the Battn.	9W
	13th	2pm	Billets. Inspection by G.O.C. 60th Bde.	8W
	14th		Billets.	9W
	15th		Billets.	

WAR DIARY or INTELLIGENCE SUMMARY

Army Form C. 2118.

(Erase heading not required.)

Place	Date	Hour	Summary of Events and Information	Remarks and references to Appendices
VERDREL	16th March	9.0 a.m.	Baln left for Vermin. Arrives at Vermin 11.0 a.m.	Shl
VERMIN	17th	6 p.m.	Baln left Vermin for trenches to relieve 1st King's Liverpool in "A" Section Calonne Sector. 3 Coys in front line. 1 Coy in support.	Shl
A Portion Calonne Sector	18th		Quiet day.	
	19th		" Lt P.T. Palmer wounded on patrol. 9 O.R. wounded	Shl
	20th		" Capt & Adjt Hon S.J.A. Lacey killed by M.G. Grenades. Capt White visiting a Sap. 3 attempts were made by Pte Green and one attempt by Capt H. Llewellyn failed to recover his body. Both afternoons recommended for immediate reward by Commanding Officer. At 7 p.m. enemy bombarded our Sap Steven under cover of which they took in Capt Lacey's body. Casualties O.R. 1 killed 3 wounded	
	21st		Quiet day. In the evening were relieved by the 11th. N.F. our Baln bivouacs into "D" Portion Bully.	Shl

Army Form C. 2118.

WAR DIARY
or
INTELLIGENCE SUMMARY.
(Erase heading not required.)

Instructions regarding War Diaries and Intelligence Summaries are contained in F. S. Regs., Part II. and the Staff Manual respectively. Title pages will be prepared in manuscript.

Place	Date	Hour	Summary of Events and Information	Remarks and references to Appendices
BOULLY.	March 22nd - 25th		50% of the Battn employed on working parties for R.Es - pioneers. On Evening of 25th. Battn relieves 11th. N.F. in "A" position CALONNE SECTOR.	Shd
"A" position	26th.		Quiet. Casualties O.R. wounded 3.	Shd
CUENNE SECTOR	27th.		During the morning Battn front line was shelled. Rest of the day quiet.	Shd
	28th.		Enemy very active with rifle grenade.	Shd
	29th.		Very quiet. During the afternoon we were relieved by 11th. N.F. and proceeded into "C" position CALONNE.	Shd
"C" position CALONNE SECTOR	30th to 31st.		Battn during these 4 days lived in cellars, employed by R.Es for working parties. On the 2nd Battn relieves 11th N.F. in "A" position CALONNE SECTOR.	Shd

A.W.
Base

23/68

Herewith the War Diary
of the 10th North'd Fusiliers
for the month of April 1916

George S. Bone
Lt & Adjt
10th North'd Fus

1-5-16

10th Natt.
Army Form C. 2118.
Feb
Vol 8
XXIV

WAR DIARY
or
INTELLIGENCE SUMMARY.
(Erase heading not required.)

Instructions regarding War Diaries and Intelligence Summaries are contained in F. S. Regs., Part II. and the Staff Manual respectively. Title pages will be prepared in manuscript.

Place	Date	Hour	Summary of Events and Information	Remarks and references to Appendices
"A" Bardion CALONNE SECTOR	3rd		Enemy very active during the 24 hrs with Rifle Grenades. At 3.30 am. 6 of the Enemy appeared on R.P. at M.20.c.5.6. Our bombers in the R.P. observed their approach & when with 20 yds threw 24 Mills Bombs Nos. 5. The hostile party threw 6 back, all of which went wide. They then retired at the double. One man was seen crawling, it is believed he was wounded by our bombs. Casualties O.R. wounded 3.	Sgd.
	4th		Enemy shells our trenches in the morning. Their bombers co-operating. Our guns & Grenadiers retaliate effectively. Casualties O.R. wounded 4.	Sgd.
	5th		Enemy active with bombs. Our artillery & Grenadiers retaliates. Casualties. C.F. Savage wounded. O.R. 2 killed 4 wounded.	Sgd.
	6th		At 9 pm 2 men Pte J.H. Scott & D. Green volunteered to place a Bangalore Torpedo in the enemy's wire. At 9 pm. on action fire So yds on the enemy's trench. after which the men went out	Sgd. 8-e

WAR DIARY
or
INTELLIGENCE SUMMARY.
(Erase heading not required.)

Army Form C. 2118.

Place	Date	Hour	Summary of Events and Information	Remarks and references to Appendices
"A" position CALONNE SECTOR	5th.		They succeeded in placing the torpedo on the enemy parapet. The Scot lit the fuse which refuses to fire. He lit another one which burns. Our own is to the "Amanal" lewis damp. At 10.30 pm Artillery fires another burst Torpedo fails to explode. At 10.30 pm Artillery fires another burst of sounds & the two men brought the torpedo in again. Both of these men displayed remarkable courage, both are recommended by Commanding Officer. See report.	Sgd.
	6th.		Quiet day. In the evening Battn. was relieved by the 11th. N.F. and proceeds in "D" position Bully. No casualties.	Sgd.
"D" position 7th. Bully 8th.			Billets. Rt. working parties. 50% employed. Billets. Rt. working parties. 50% Employed.	Sgd. Sgd.

WAR DIARY
or
INTELLIGENCE SUMMARY.
(Erase heading not required.)

Army Form C. 2118.

Place	Date	Hour	Summary of Events and Information	Remarks and references to Appendices
"D" position Bully.	April 9th		BILLETS. R.E. working parties. 50% employed. 19447. R.D. Grew awarded military medal for conduct on night of 29th March 1916.	AH
	10th		BILLETS. R.E. working parties. 50% employed.	Shd
			Between 1 p.m. & 4 p.m. our artillery bombarded German 1st & 2nd line trenches. There was no retaliation on our trenches. Relief from 6 to 11th April.	Shd
A position Calonne Sgoor.	11		Relieved 11th N.F. in "A" position. On howitzer battery retaliated at 10.30 p.m. On hostile arty. between 10 a.m. & 10.30 p.m. Equivalent to hostile arty.	Shd
"	12th		Enemy shells during the forenoon. No damage done. Our artillery fire was opened on our front line & at 1 p.m. again.	Shd

Army Form C. 2118.

WAR DIARY
or
INTELLIGENCE SUMMARY.
(Erase heading not required.)

Instructions regarding War Diaries and Intelligence Summaries are contained in F.S. Regs., Part II. and the Staff Manual respectively. Title pages will be prepared in manuscript.

Place	Date	Hour	Summary of Events and Information	Remarks and references to Appendices
"A" Section CALONNE SECTOR	13th.	9 p.m.	One torpedo gun fire 5 rds at enemys Sap. N. 21. a. 1. 7. Shooting was accurate & much damage was done 1934. Enemy inactive all day. Ours now: a hope Scot & hope Davidson accessway wounded by premature explosion of rifle grenade. Enemy places on tinware at intervals during day and N 19 of the 14th. At 9. am the bombardments was at its height, to damage of much importance was done. Sgt. J. B. Senn awarded D.C.M. for conduct on 5.4.16 have Cpl. Springer & 2 men killed & 7 wounded at STAND-TO by German snipers.	Shd.
"	14th.			Shd.
"	15th.		Pte Pennie E. bikes wounds. Relieved by 11 N.F. 2293 Re proceeds to "C" Position CALONNE.	Shd.
"G" Position CALONNE	16. 17 18		Bath. provides R.E. Working parties. Relieved by 18t Kings Liverpool at 4 p.m. 18th and proceed to NERGNIN arriving in billets	Shd.

Army Form C. 2118.

WAR DIARY
or
INTELLIGENCE SUMMARY.
(Erase heading not required.)

Instructions regarding War Diaries and Intelligence Summaries are contained in F. S. Regs., Part II. and the Staff Manual respectively. Title pages will be prepared in manuscript.

Place	Date	Hour	Summary of Events and Information	Remarks and references to Appendices
HERSIN	19.	2 a.m.	Batln arrived in billets.	Shl
"	20.		R.E. working parties same in Souchez Sector.	Shl
"	21.			
"	22.		Batln baths refitted.	
"	23.			
"	24.		21st 160 men inoculated.	
"	25.		22nd 100 " "	
"	26.		Batln moves to DINION. leaving billets at 9.30 am arrive DINION at 1 p.m.	
DINION	27.		300 men employed on working parties. 100 men inoculated. 1944? M.O.s Queen awards D.C.M. for Cpl Wilson 5th R.N.	R.
"	28.			
"	29.		Batln attends San Devon Kaboir. 100 men inoculated	Shl
"	30.		Church Parade.	

George F. Branw.
Lt. / Agt. 10th N.F.

#353 Wt. W3544/1454 700,000 5/15 D. D. & L.   A.D.S.S./Forms/C. 2118.

AG
3rd Echelon

23/68

Herewith is the War
Diary of the 10 North'd Fus
for the month of May 1916

J Wenies Major
Cmdg 10 North Fus

ORDERLY ROOM
6 JUN. 1916
10th (Ser.) Bn. Northumberland Fusiliers

WAR DIARY
or
INTELLIGENCE SUMMARY.

Army Form C. 2118.

(Erase heading not required.)

Instructions regarding War Diaries and Intelligence Summaries are contained in F. S. Regs., Part II. and the Staff Manual respectively. Title pages will be prepared in manuscript.

Place	Date MAY.	Hour	Summary of Events and Information	Remarks and references to Appendices
DIVION.	1st/2nd		NIL.	
	3rd		L/Sergt. D. Green was presented with D.C.M. & M.M. Alberts Pte G.W. Scott with D.C.M. Ribbon by G.O.C. 1st Army. General Munro.	
	5th	8am	Bann marched to billets in Monchy au bois LAIRES	
		3.30pm	Arrived at LAIRES.	
	6th		Battn carried on Battn Schemes took part in 3 Batt Scheme.	
	/10th		Work has been impeded by inclemency of the weather.	
	20th	6am	Battn marched to FERNES. And ratiOned at 11-57. Left Arriving at BARLIN	
		13.47.	marched to VERDREL and relieved 19th London Regt.	
	21st	7pm	marched to trenches relieving 2nd Sth Lanc. Regt in SOUCHEZ I	
SOUCHEZ. I.			position. Very quiet night.	
	22nd	3/9am	Bombardment on VIMY RIDGE commenced & was kept up	16122 Gnl Pte S Cragg wounded.
	23rd		intermittently. to our 22nd. There was little shelling on the Battn Front.	

Army Form C. 2118.

WAR DIARY
or
INTELLIGENCE SUMMARY.
(Erase heading not required.)

Instructions regarding War Diaries and Intelligence Summaries are contained in F.S. Regs., Part II. and the Staff Manual respectively. Title pages will be prepared in manuscript.

Place	Date	Hour	Summary of Events and Information	Remarks and references to Appendices
SOUCHEZ I	May 29th	9 pm	An Explosion was heard in LENS. Report was clearly heard. Flames seen.	5295 Replies 25th announced SMt
-do-	24th		Little Artillery activity. One Coy in SOUCHEZ Stn. was shelled from 8pm-12pm. No damage was done.	10625 Rope hangar 24th just opened. Rope removed. SMt
-do-	25th		Very Quiet day. Relieved by 14th A.P. in "A" position at midnight without a hitch.	24th 20505 taken over SMt
NOTRE DAME DE LORETTE Defences "C" position	26th		"C" position. NOTRE DAME de LORETTE Defences. On the whole the situation was quiet. On the 27th our left Coy "B" Coy was shelled between 4pm and 6pm about 40 shells burst in the Aug. and vic. No damage was done.	SMt
-do-	29th		Working parties here employed mainly in "C" position improving Battn + Aug. On line trenches were supplied to RE's for work on DIAGONAL Support line.	SMt

Army Form C. 2118.

WAR DIARY
or
INTELLIGENCE SUMMARY.
(Erase heading not required.)

Instructions regarding War Diaries and Intelligence Summaries are contained in F.S. Regs., Part II. and the Staff Manual respectively. Title pages will be prepared in manuscript.

Place	Date	Hour	Summary of Events and Information	Remarks and references to Appendices
Notre Dame Defence "C" position	30th		We were relieved by 11th N.Z. and proceeded to "A" position.	SM. Sd
	31 st		Somme 1. NIL.	

Geof. Bain
Lt Maditz
Lt Nostio: Pl—

#353 Wt W2544/1454 700,000 5/15 D.D. & L. A.D.S.S./Forms/C. 2118.

WAR DIARY or INTELLIGENCE SUMMARY

(Erase heading not required.)

Army Form C. 2118.

10 North Fus
10" N.F. Vol 10
June 1916

Place	Date	Hour	Summary of Events and Information	Remarks and references to Appendices
Souchez	June Sunday 1st	4 p.m.	Our Artillery commenced a very heavy bombardment of Vimy Ridge which continued until	Casualties
		9 p.m.	when 2 min. was enforced apparently by an intense intermittent bombardment was a steady shelling. After some intense bombardment by Bosche R.E. working parties went down, but had to return with 2 casualties.	1989 Cpl A. Davies wounded 1970 L.C. a Conti 10015 Pte R. Hunan
	2.		Quiet at 9 p.m. 2 Lt A.S. Calder taken over the strength. Enemy's Artillery and Mortars were active on the Railway front. Some damage done. R.E. working parties supplied.	Cas. B
		7.30am	Lt. E. Lombardes and Mess assistants went Mortars. No damage was done. R.E. work parties supplied.	Casualties wounded 9246 Lt J Driver 10755 Sgt Adamson 2326 J Williams
	3rd		Enemy was quiet. B.O.L.I. on our left in Souchez II relieved enemy's trenches 15th Recruit Draft of 120 R. arrived. R.E. work parties supplied.	Ref.
	4th		Quiet day. Relieved as High Bn. 111 N.F. & proceeded to "D" position in Noulette Wood	Ref.
"D" position Noulette Wood	5th 6th 7th 8th 9th		Working parties for R.E. & carrying parties supplied.	Ref.

Army Form C. 2118.

WAR DIARY
or
INTELLIGENCE SUMMARY.
(Erase heading not required.)

Instructions regarding War Diaries and Intelligence Summaries are contained in F. S. Regs., Part II. and the Staff Manual respectively. Title pages will be prepared in manuscript.

Place	Date	Hour	Summary of Events and Information	Remarks and references to Appendices
"B" Section Reserve	9th	10 am	Bahn was billeted by 11th to proceed at 6 pm to proceed to VERDREL	Sub.
VERDREL	10th		Col. A.S. Stewart relinquishes command of Bahn & proceeds to England. Major G.M. Rohan took over temporary command of the Bahn.	Sub.
"	11th		Bahn relieved by 17th London & proceed to DIEVAL by road.	Sub.
DIEVAL	12th		Bahn marches to CREPY. 9000 litres.	
CREPY	13th		Coy Parade. New canvas Out.	Sub.
"	14th		"	Sub.
"	15th		"	
DENNEBROEUCQ	16th		Bahn marches to DENNEBROEUCQ. Excellent accommodation.	Sub.
"	16th		Bahn training	Sub.
"	17th		Bahn training. On manoeuvre grounds	Sub.
"	18th		Roe " "	
"	19th		Divine Service. Major Lord R. Manners D.S.O. (Res. of Off.) becomes temporary Commander of the Bahn	Sub.
"	20		Bahn (Coy parade).	
"	21st		Bahn & Roe training on manoeuvre grounds.	Sub.

Army Form C. 2118.

WAR DIARY
or
INTELLIGENCE SUMMARY.
(Erase heading not required.)

Instructions regarding War Diaries and Intelligence Summaries are contained in F. S. Regs., Part II. and the Staff Manual respectively. Title pages will be prepared in manuscript.

Place	Date	Hour	Summary of Events and Information	Remarks and references to Appendices
DERNANCOURT	22.		Coy Parade. Gen inspection	Sgd.
"	23.		"	
"	24.	noon.	Batn marches to AIRE entrains at 7.29 pm	Sgd.
PICQUIGNY	25.		Detrains at LONGPRÉ at 3.45 am & marches to PICQUIGNY. Arriving there 9 am. No work done during the rest of the day.	
"	26.	10am	C.O. inspects the Bathes &c. Coy Parade in the afternoon.	Sgd.
"	27.		Coy Parades.	
"	28.		Orders were received to move to BOUZINCOURT. Light parade were conducted.	Sgd.
"	29.		Coy Parade.	Sgd. 6 INF.
"	30.		Batn moves to BOUZINCOURT at 11 pm by road.	Sgd.

68th Inf.Bde.
23rd Div.

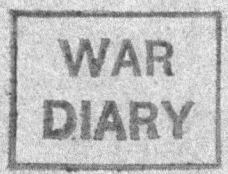

10th BATTN. THE NORTHUMBERLAND FUSILIERS.

J U L Y

1 9 1 6

Army Form C. 2118.

10th North. Fus. 68/23

WAR DIARY or INTELLIGENCE SUMMARY.

(Erase heading not required.)

Instructions regarding War Diaries and Intelligence Summaries are contained in F.S. Regs., Part II. and the Staff Manual respectively. Title pages will be prepared in manuscript.

Place	Date July	Hour	Summary of Events and Information	Remarks and references to Appendices
BOUAINVILLE	1st		Batn "Stood by". Coy parades in the morning. Orders received at 6.30pm to move to FRANVILLERS.	Nil.
FRANVILLERS	2nd	8.20pm	Marches to FRANVILLERS	
		1am	Arrives in billets. "Stood by" for the day. Billets fair.	Nil.
		7.45pm	Batn parades off for bivouac at MILLENCOURT.	
		8pm	Marches off for bivouac at MILLENCOURT.	
		11.45pm	Arrives in bivouac field. Ground very wet.	
MILLENCOURT	3rd	3pm	Marches to Reserve trenches. Johnson Reserve Officer. Coy left the Batn 6 Remain with transport. Major Rohan, Capt Shia, Lt Jacob Y.Shia. Rain commenced at 7pm & continued through the night.	Nil.
Reserve trenches ALBERT		6.30pm	Arrives at trenches.	
	4th	10am	Inspection of lines by C.O.	
BECOURT		2pm	Marches to BECOURT bivouacs in the wood. Very wet.	
		2pm	Orders received to relieve the troops to Reserve trenches.	Nil.
Reserve trenches ALBERT		10pm	Arrives back at Reserve trenches along Run orbial ALBERT	

8353 Wt. W2544/1454 700,000 5/15 D.D. & L. A.D.S.S./Forms/C. 2118.

Army Form C. 2118.

WAR DIARY or **INTELLIGENCE SUMMARY.**

(Erase heading not required.)

Instructions regarding War Diaries and Intelligence Summaries are contained in F. S. Regs., Part II and the Staff Manual respectively. Title pages will be prepared in manuscript.

Place	Date	Hour	Summary of Events and Information	Remarks and references to Appendices
Becourt Wood	July 5.	2.30 p.m.	Bn moves to Becourt Wood to support attack on Horseshoe Trench by 69th Bde.	
Becourt Wood		5 p.m.	Arrived & bivouacs in Becourt Wood.	
		5.15 p.m.	"A" Coy moves up to Heligoland to support 9th Yorks.	SM
		8.30 p.m.	"B" " " " " " Scotts Redoubt.	
			News received that 69th has obtained their objective & taken 175 prisoners.	
		9 p.m.	50 men from "C" at Coy Hqrs in Shelter Reserve. Remainder in Bady of 9th I.A.	
	6th	10 a.m.	Bn (less "A" & "B" Coys) moves to Heligoland. On arrival at Heligoland ordered to move to Scotts Redoubt to relieve	
Scotts Redoubt			9th Yorks. Causes the two Coys in Scotts Redoubt shelled on our Bn.	SM
		11 p.m.	Relief reports: There has Constant shelling throughout the day — & was intense at 11 p.m.	

Army Form C. 2118.

WAR DIARY
or
INTELLIGENCE SUMMARY.
(Erase heading not required.)

Instructions regarding War Diaries and Intelligence Summaries are contained in F.S. Regs., Part II. and the Staff Manual respectively. Title pages will be prepared in manuscript.

Place	Date	Hour	Summary of Events and Information	Remarks and references to Appendices
Scots Redoubt	6.		"B" Coy has shelter leaving as about the lines about some distance. The weather has been beginning to fill up.	SH
		11 p.m.	60 men employed carrying bombs to a Welsh Regt. who were on our immediate left: some 5000 bombs were carried up.	
	7.	1 a.m.	All available men helped with the carrying of bombs under the supervision of 2/Lt. Josten. The B.O. Strongpoint to War about 1500 bombs were carried up to the Front line to help in the Divisional attack. During the commencement ordered Bosche stores	
		9.30 a.m.	Bombardment throughout the night was fierce. 12 D.L.I. during the dark hours who had relieved 12 D.L.I. during the dark hours attacked the enemy line about Bailiff Wood. The bombardment was intense for 40 mins before the attack proper left, the line. The Battn. front was subjected to retaliation from the enemy trenches by this time. were in a hopeless condition thus his peace. Accp Whein nearer impeded the evacuation of the casualties.	SH

Army Form C. 2118.

WAR DIARY
or
INTELLIGENCE SUMMARY.
(Erase heading not required.)

Instructions regarding War Diaries and Intelligence Summaries are contained in F.S. Regs., Part II and the Staff Manual respectively. Title pages will be prepared in manuscript.

Place	Date	Hour	Summary of Events and Information	Remarks and references to Appendices
Scots Redoubt	7		On "D"Coy front was subjected to heavy artillery fire throughout the morning.	
		12 noon	Our Lewis moved to the S.E. Corner of the Redoubt and the Bomb Parties the 12th D.L.I. who moved up with the first line.	Sgd
		4 p.m.	12 R.S.L. Attacks Lonely from line which was occupied.	
		12.20 am	Lewis moves back to its former position in S.W. Cr. of the Redoubt. Reviews have been much compels. Great difficulty has experienced in the evacuation of the wounded. Stretchers on the day surface. Carrying parties were collected who were working without cease up to the front line. It is most like unusual. Our wire transports the day were	
		4 p.m.	She has been subjected to heavy artillery fire. By this line the men were commencing to suffer from trench foot.	Sgd

Army Form. C. 2118.

WAR DIARY
or
INTELLIGENCE SUMMARY.

(Erase heading not required.)

Instructions regarding War Diaries and Intelligence Summaries are contained in F.S. Regs., Part II. and the Staff Manual respectively. Title pages will be prepared in manuscript.

Place	Date	Hour	Summary of Events and Information	Remarks and references to Appendices
SCOTTS REDOUBT	8.		Several men & 2/Lt M.G. Elwes have been sent on to the 3rd Ambulance suffering from Trench Complaint.	
		4pm.	1/6th. D.L.I. attempted to obtain a footing in BAILIFF WOOD= our Coy moved up into position vacated by 10 Bn.9. If heavy barrage had been put up over our Trenches and communicating trenches. The operation has commenced. The men brought in considerably a new line commenced. The men by now were suffering more with exposure & trench foot. With the continual movement there was little chance for the trench to harden.	Jul
	9.		There was nothing to report except shelling to which we replied. Rain has been falling by 2 Coys. 11 N.F. afterwards 9.48 am. "B" & "D" Coys were relieved in RECORD WOOD= Bivouac in RECORD WOOD=	Jul

2353 Wt. W2544/1454 700,000 5/15 D. D. & L. A.D.S.S./Forms/C. 2118.

Army Form C. 2118.

WAR DIARY
or
INTELLIGENCE SUMMARY.
(Erase heading not required.)

Place	Date	Hour	Summary of Events and Information	Remarks and references to Appendices
SCOTTS REDOUBT	9/13th	Midnight	The relief of the Battn by NZ has been completed & Bn moves to bivouacs in BECOURT WOOD.	Our losses connection for the 5 days have 145 are chiefly due to Congested state of trenches and the difficulty of providing cover. Orders to continue movement of the Corps from one position to another. In respect of the affairs attack Reference of the new area. Areas being circumstances browning operation.
BECOURT	10 - 10.20am		Marches to billets in ALBERT.	
ALBERT			Men allowed to rest & clean up.	
ALBERT	11th		Rott - Car at 10.30am C.O. inspects billets at 12 noon.	
"	12th		Battn now in Reserve to 34th Division	
"	13th	10am	" " " " C.O. inspects the Battn.	
"	"	12noon	" " " "	
"	"	3pm	" " " "	
"	Rest	"	" " " "	
"	15th	3.30am	Order received to proceed to SUSA-TARA Line & support attack by 34th Division.	
		9.15am	Battn marches on off ALBERT. Took up position in the Reserve line at 10 am.	

Army Form C. 2118.

WAR DIARY
or
INTELLIGENCE SUMMARY.

(Erase heading not required.)

Instructions regarding War Diaries and Intelligence Summaries are contained in F.S. Regs., Part II. and the Staff Manual respectively. Title pages will be prepared in manuscript.

Place	Date July.	Hour	Summary of Events and Information	Remarks and references to Appendices
USNA-TARA Reserve LINE	16.	11 a.m.	"C" & "D" Coys moves up to support line near the CRATER. to take over from Bth K.R.R.C. the remaining 2 Coys Bivouacs in rear of Reserve line.	
			The day was quiet & nothing of importance happened.	
		11.45 p.m.	"C" & "D" Coys returns to Reserve line.	
	16		Battn remains in Bivouac in rear of USNA-TARA LINE.	
	17		Orders received to attack POZIÈRES. & the Battn hold until 9 p.m.	
		9 p.m.	Battn moves up to relieve D.L.I. Who has been ordered to take enemys first line. On the outskirts of POZIÈRES.	
			During the march up Sausage Valley enemy put up a heavy barrage. but fortunately no Casualties.	
		11 p.m.	Arrived at CHALK PIT & leave D.L.I. has failed to take their objective. On orders from hrs to take over the exact line from D.L.I. Battn has getting rapidly into position.	
			Attack the Dam objective at zero.	

WAR DIARY or INTELLIGENCE SUMMARY

Army Form C. 2118.

Place	Date	Hour	Summary of Events and Information	Remarks and references to Appendices
Near POZIÈRES	18.8.	9 a.m.	The Operation was carried out. Works had on Consolidation. The Shelling up to this hour was heavy: but towards dawn it slackened.	
			Throughout the morning there was little to report beyond intermittent shelling of our line. The Cmdg Offr visited Coys & when opportunity offered the Coy'rs themselves. Arm. continues on Consolidation.	
		1 p.m.	D Coys line was subjected to heavy fire from the hostile "heavies" on Jun's Gun also between two batteries up an advance position suffers heavily. 2 men were killed. Our wounded while our line destroyed dug-outs completely.	
			This bombardment on our line lasted until "Stand-To" next morning.	
		7 p.m.	H Ration parties set off for GORDON DUMP. On the way down came under heavy shell fire. 1 N.C.O. two killed 10 O.R. wounded.	

WAR DIARY or INTELLIGENCE SUMMARY

Army Form C. 2118.

(Erase heading not required.)

Place	Date	Hour	Summary of Events and Information	Remarks and references to Appendices
Hunters Men POZIÈRES	18	9.30pm	Officer patrol have been sent out from our lines to reconnoitre the German trench opposite our kitchen Mound. On whether owing to bombs along to the trench join up with 1st Divn. Lt.E. Lawrence two Officer Charge of the operation. Cpl Agnew "A" Co. 4th Bat. Clarke of the patrol came back at 11 pm. Obtained information with M Guns. It seems this information German line has no longer in known occupation from Baw. that 1st Divn.	
	19	12 mn	During however on our night operation two Sergts canceled patrols under Lt. Robin Brown Garia doing with 9th have Rogers on our Left. C.O. and Anzac Redin arrived closed over. On the Shoe Pit Day two Officers Crust! the Anzac. here On the row up their guns had Quinn like trenches	Casualties during the 48 hr. Order Lt Renshaw wounded Lt Lt 2 Hussars - 35 wounded
		10.30am	German trench set up a green Rocket. A strong barrage was at once put up behind our lines. Which however did but little the relief.	
	20.	1 am.	The Relief of the Battn by 2nd Divn. Anzac has Confirmed. The moved to billets in ALBERT.	

Army Form C. 2118.

WAR DIARY
or
INTELLIGENCE SUMMARY.
(Erase heading not required.)

Instructions regarding War Diaries and Intelligence Summaries are contained in F. S. Regs., Part II. and the Staff Manual respectively. Title pages will be prepared in manuscript.

Place	Date	Hour	Summary of Events and Information	Remarks and references to Appendices
Franvillers	21	4 am.	Relief was complete & the Bn. has arrived in ALBERT billets.	
		9 am.	marched to FRANVILLERS. Arrived there at 1 pm.	
	22.		Coy. Parades.	
"	23.		Coy. Parades. Major General Babington Cmndg 23rd Divn presented Military Medals to following men for good work done in Recto Redoubt 6th - 10th July 1916. 16/10/1916 Pte Stole J. 16126 " Knapp W. 10778 " Toilet J. 7011 hope Cpl. McQueen 10390 Pte. R.W. Clarke 16076 " A. Wilson.	925/ 518
	23.		Coy. Recreation Church Parade.	
	24.		Coy. Parade. Coy men Baths.	
"	25.	11:30am	III Corps Commander inspects & thanks of 6th Bde.	
"	26.	9.15	Battn marches to trenches between POZIERES & BAZENTIN-LE-PETIT. Bivouaced en route at Albert from 1pm - 6pm.	

#353 Wt. W2544/1454 700,000 5/15 D. D. & L. A.D.S.S./Forms/C. 2118.

Army Form. C. 2118.

WAR DIARY
or
INTELLIGENCE SUMMARY.
(Erase heading not required.)

9248

Place	Date	Hour	Summary of Events and Information	Remarks and references to Appendices
Rivonne nr ALBERT	26	6 p.m.	Marches off to trenches.	
Trenches between POZIÈRES and BAZENTIN-LE-PETIT	27	11 p.m.	Bttn had arrived in trenches; but owing to a bombing fight in MUNSTER ALLEY the relief of 2nd Welch was not complete until 3 a.m. The Bazenton Howitzer Artillery was very active during the relief but towards dawn quieted down. During the night all men were employed on consolidation. The Anzacs on our left gave much resistance to our Bombers in MUNSTER ALLEY where the Germans were offering a strong resistance.	
		2 a.m.	Carrying parties were bringing up bombs & S.A.A. throughout the night. Their parties were supplied by Battns in Support. The morning was fairly quiet but towards noon hostile shelling increased. Several men of the 2 platoons digging in LANCS TRENCH were buried but successfully dug out again	

#353 Wt. W2544/1454 700,000 5/15 D. D. & L. A.D.S.S./Forms/C. 2118.

Army Form C.2118.

WAR DIARY
OR
INTELLIGENCE SUMMARY.
(Erase heading not required.)

10 N. Fus Vol 11

Place	Date	Hour	Summary of Events and Information	Remarks and references to Appendices
Trenches	26.27		During the afternoon O.C. B. Coy. 1. Came up to take over trenches. 2 Coys were relieved by days, 2 by night.	Shel
		9 p.m.	Relief was Complete: Our Casualties during the 20 hours from line amounts to 50 O.R.: Major Parkin CMG a/c Con	Shel
		11 p.m.	Two wounded in the head on the morning of 27th. Rain had arrived in Scotts Redoubt When it renewed until 4 p.m. When relieved by 9th Yorks: Regt. Nothing of	Shel
	28.		importance occurred during the 24 hrs in Reserve:	Shel
ALBERT	29.	6 p.m.	Baan had arrived in billets in ALBERT: Coy Parade.	Shel
"	30.		Voluntary Church Service:	Shel
	31.		Coy Parade.	

R Manners Lieut Col
C/mdg 10t N.F.

9224

68th Brigade.
23rd Division.

1/10th BATTALION

NORTHUMBERLAND FUSILIERS

AUGUST 1 9 1 6

Report on Raid 30/31st.

Army Form C. 2118.

WAR DIARY
or
INTELLIGENCE SUMMARY.
(Erase heading not required.)

10 N. Fus
Vol. 12

Place	Date	Hour	Summary of Events and Information	Remarks and references to Appendices
ALBERT	Aug 1st	2 pm	Our howitzers burst shells opposite the Church in ALBERT. 9 horses were killed (6 H.D. + 3 H.D.) 6 men killed + 5 wounded.	A.
CONTALMAISON	2nd	2 pm	Rain makes off ! Take over trenches from 11 N. YORKS in CONTALMAISON. Working parties busy repairing during the night. On relief C.O. Lieut. Col. Roper-Dunn taken over.	A.
"	2nd		Our position was shelled intermittently. Shells of YORKSHIRE ALLEY. Thompson the day. Enemy's two shots burst at the entrance to Major Auerons' Coy. dug-out. Trench MARTIN & Caygin fairly quiet.	A.
"	3rd		Wounding to enemy - nothing to importance to report.	
"	3rd	2 pm	Majors G. Malcolm, Robson 2nd i/c & Capt Dodd have taken ALBERT by their left CONTALMAISON. Relieving B.D. 25th in front of their trenches.	A.
Trenches		4 pm	X. 6. d. 5. 9 to X. 5. b. 7. 8½. Quiet relief.	94f
		6.30 pm	Relief complete.	8B

WAR DIARY
or
INTELLIGENCE SUMMARY
(Erase heading not required.)

Army Form C. 2118.

Place	Date	Hour	Summary of Events and Information	Remarks and references to Appendices
Peuvelee	3rd	9.30pm	Enemy commenced bombardment of our Back Area being at time became intense. Our Artillery fire shell on MUNSTER ALLEY =) Through this he supposed 2 Canadian CSM super "A" Coy has both legs almost blown off. to whom honour be shortly afterwards succumbed.	Sd/
"	4th	2.30pm	Bombardment opened down. Strong he any enemy guns:) opposite GLORIER ==? our snipers accounted for 4 Germans in the gap opposite and in the repair of MARTIN PUICH.	
		12 noon	Our Coy "A" is here relieved by 2 Coy B D.L.I. "B" Coy remains in support operations on B S.I. at M high = Ruth Hope 2 our hours on to hinder in CONTALMAISON. 2 Coys 16 Bn Rivin Rey been there about 6 o—	Sd/

927

WAR DIARY
INTELLIGENCE SUMMARY.
(Erase heading not required.)

Army Form C. 2118.

Place	Date	Hour	Summary of Events and Information	Remarks and references to Appendices
CONTALMAISON	Aug 4th	3 pm	Relief now complete.	
		9.15 pm	B.A.L.I. and Australians on our left commences two attack	
			"C" Coy 10th K.R.R. moves up to reinforce line "A" Coy 15th R.F.	
		10.45 pm	moves up to take the place of "C" Coy 10 KRR.	
			From 9.15 pm - 5.12 midnight the enemy bombardment was a fire	
			bombardment. The enemy maintained throughout the majority of his shells being S. of Pozières down the Albert Crack.	SA
		5th 4am	2 Captn CONTALMAISON + 2nd 15 KRRO. been relieved by 11th Royal Fusiliers	
			2 Coy. A.R. proceeds to Albert in ALBERT. Arriving here.	
			C. Coy 8a 11 Bn "C" Coy arrived in Albert + ALBERT.	
			Total Casualties for this action 3/5th August. 1 off killed. 1 wounded, 2nd R. Norman, 2nd R. - 6 killed 18 wounded	Major Bellew, Major Newman

9287

Army Form C. 2113.

WAR DIARY
or
INTELLIGENCE SUMMARY.
(Erase heading not required.)

Place	Date	Hour	Summary of Events and Information	Remarks and references to Appendices
ALBERT	5th/		Show has intimated Shelling of the town of ALBERT	
	6th		throughout the night. Said to be the heaviest ever on Advance began. Guns of Calibres up to 6" have fired nils us = Throwers no Casualties.	
		6pm	Owing to the shelling on the right of 5th to 6th Augt + 9t5. Grain has premises for the Batn. to proceed to Coronas in TARA VALLEY + take up remains in ALBERTA	
TARA VALLEY	7th		Advance party sent on to LA HOUSSOYE.	
	8th	9am	Relieved by 8th Brdrs Seaforth Here + proceeded by Rous to LA HOUSSOYE.	

Army Form C. 2118.

WAR DIARY
or
INTELLIGENCE SUMMARY.
(Erase heading not required.)

9301

Place	Date	Hour	Summary of Events and Information	Remarks and references to Appendices
LAHOUSSOYE	8	Noon	Arrived in billets at LAHOUSSOYS.	JB
"	9th.		Coy. parade.	
"	10th.	3pm.	Transport moved by road to POULAINVILLE en route to GORENFLOS.	JB
	11th.	10 am.	Bath. Marched to entraining Stn at FRECHENCOURT. Entrainment delayed from 11.30am to 5pm. Arrived at LONGPRE at	
		10pm.	Marched to GORENFLOS. Transport marched from POULAINVILLE to GORENFLOS.	JB
GORENFLOS	12th.	2.30am	Arrived GORENFLOS.	
		3pm	Transport marches to entraining Stn LONGPRE.	
"		6pm	Rain " " "	
		9.11pm	" Entrained.	
		10.30pm	Train left for BAILLEUL via ABBEVILLE, ETAPLES.	
	13.	7.30am	Arrived at BAILLEUL & marched to billets at S.O.3.6. near FLETRE	

Army Form C. 2118.

WAR DIARY
or
INTELLIGENCE SUMMARY.
(Erase heading not required.)

9318

Place	Date	Hour	Summary of Events and Information	Remarks and references to Appendices
FLETRE. W.S.a.3.6.13. Billets:	13.	11.30am	Arrived in Billets. "C" Coy remains at detachm'n Sw a a Fatigue Party - occupying billets in BAILLEUL Overnight 13/14 = Coy parades:	SB
"	14.	1.30pm	Marches from FLETRE to STEENWERCK. Arrive at destination at 5 p.m. Good billets:	SB
STEENWERCK	15.	6.30pm	Marches from STEENWERCK to LE BIZET. Arriving 1oth R.W.KENTS., 123 Bde at Queens at 11.25 p.m.	SB
LE BIZET.	16.	9 p.m	Commences the relief of 10th Queens: 123 Bde in trenches = relief complete by 11.30 p.m.	SB
LEFT SUBSID'y Redoubts LE BOCQUET Trenches	17.		Very quiet day. G.O.C. 68th Bde B.G. K. Page Croft, Brigade gave over Command of the Bde to A.G. G.N. Colville. D.S.O.	SB
"	19.		Nothing to report:	

Army Form C. 2118.

WAR DIARY
or
INTELLIGENCE SUMMARY.
(Erase heading not required.)

9728

Place	Date	Hour	Summary of Events and Information	Remarks and references to Appendices
Left Suburb of Armentières LE TOUQUET TRENCHES	August 24		The period is known to be exceedingly quiet. Area is nothing of importance to report. On 22nd No. 23958 Rifleman "B" Coy was killed whilst on sentry duty in front line by enemy machine gun fire.	JB
"D" Section ARMENTIÈRES & LE BIZET	25		Saw Battn was relieved by 11 N.9 in front trenches & proceeded to Armentières 2 Coy's Barn hospital in ARMENTIÈRES 2 Coys LE BIZET. Special party of 2 offs & 30 O.R. commenced training for the raid.	JB
	26	"	working parties:	
	27	"	"	
	28	"	Lt. R. Cruikshank who however on failure reconnoitring the ground for the raid. Lt. Loraine J.O. took McMichan's place in the party.	

#353 Wt W2544/1454 700,000 5/15 D. D. & L. A.D.S.S./Forms/C. 2118.

WAR DIARY
INTELLIGENCE SUMMARY

Army Form C. 2118.

Place	Date	Hour	Summary of Events and Information	Remarks and references to Appendices
"Dugout" ARMENTIERES	29th		Working parties. The rain khiew has to have been made on this day two postpones owing to the time being no known direction for the Gas khien two being used in Co-operation :-	SB
" LE BIZET	30th		Working parties -	
	31st	1.30 a.m.	Gas has released along the Divre front. At 3.15 am after own intense bombardment our raiding party of 2 off 35 men went over :- for particulars see Appendix. Rain supplies the same R.E. working parties :-	SB 9324

F.M. Morris
Cmdg. 10th Welsh Rs.

MINOR OPERATION ORDER NO. 62.   29/8/16.   7804

1. The Battalion will furnish a strong patrol of 2 Officers and 35 other ranks, to act in connection with a combined gas and Artillery operation, which will be undertaken by the Corps tonight.

2. <u>Intention.</u>
(a) To note the effects of the Gas and Artillery on the enemys personnel and defences.
(b) To kill as many Germans as possible and secure one or more prisoners.
(c) To remove or destroy any Machine Guns found within the limits of the objective.
(d) To secure identification proofs.

3. <u>Objective.</u> Enemys front line trench from C.4.a.8½.½ to C.4.d.8½.8½.

4. <u>Composition.</u> 2nd Lt. E.Lawrence (in command) and 17 other ranks of "B" Coy.
2nd Lieut. J.P.Lorains and 18 other ranks of "C" Coy.

5. <u>Method of attack.</u> At 2.30 a.m. the patrol will leave "Dead end", "C" Coy. leading, and file along the ditch in front of our wire, halt and lie down at two paces interval between men and 30 paces between the two companies, thus forming two parties.
At 2.35 a.m. the patrol will advance, the left party via Crater to the 2 weak places (C and D) in enemys wire, the right party to gap in enemys wire on right (e).
The left party will hold C.T. "Y" with three bombers, three bayonet men and one N.C.O. and junction of C.T. and Fire trench.
1 N.C.O. and 1 bomber and 1 bayonet man will hold C.T. "O" about 20 yards from its junction with fire trench.
2nd Lieut. Lawrence and 5 men will clear trench up to "W".
The right party will hold C.T. "P" with 1 N.C.O. 3 Bombers and 3 Bayonet men at its junction with fire trench.
2 men will clear "Dead end" at :N".
The remainder under 2nd Lieut. Lorains will clear the trench to "W".
1 man in each party will be detailed to secure Identifications; 2 men to take charge of prisoners.
On the signal (by whistle) to withdraw all men will immediately leave the trench and will withdraw to ditch "A" & "B" along which they will creep back to "Dead end".
In the event of the whistle not being heard, all men are to withdraw at 12 minutes after start, at which time a bugle on our parapet will sound a succession of "G's".

6. Watches will be synchronised at 12.30 a.m. 30th inst.

7. <u>Medical.</u> Capt. C.K.McKerrow R.A.M.C. will establish an Advance Dressing Station in Cellar at ESSEX ~~TRXXCH TRENCHX~~ CENTRAL. Two stretcher bearers from "B" and two from "C" will be at CELLAR at ESSEX CENTRAL and MONMOUTH HOUSE respectively.
Battalion report centre ESSEX CENTRAL Cellar from 12.30 a.m. to 3 a.m.

     Signed. R,Manners. Lt Colonel.
     Commanding 10th Northumberland Fusiliers.

Communicated to all concerned.
1.30 p.m. 29th inst.

ACCOUNT OF RAID CARRIED OUT ON NIGHT OF 30/31 August '16.

1. Orders for the attack and explanatory sketch are attached.

2. The raiders who were organised in two parties each consisting of 1 Officer and 18 other ranks marched from their quarters in LYS FARM at 11 p.m. and were accomodated in cellars at ESSEX CENTRAL and MONMOUTH HOUSE during the gas attack and preliminary bombardment. The raiding party was considerably delayed at starting, owing to the MONMOUTH HOUSE party coming under shell fire on their way to the place of exit. Sergt. Rayment was buried by the explosion of a shell and was unable to take part in the raid.
The party left our trench and entered the starting ditch without any trouble or casualties. The start was delayed owing to Very Lights being fired from our parapet near our right flank, a runner was sent to stop this.
At 3.15 a.m. the party moved quickly forward on the signal being given and got about 30 yards over "No Man's Land" at the double when, owing to Very Lights from our own and enemys trenches it was deemed advisable to crawl.
The left party, under 2nd Lieut. E.Lawrence, got to the enemys wire unperceived and the left portion of it were getting through the gap when they were assailed by rifle fire and bombs.
The raiders retaliated getting a good number of bombs into the enemys trench, from which cries and groans could be heard.
2nd Lieut. E.Lawrence was here struck by a splinter of a bomb, but was able to continue in charge.
The right half of the left party could not get to their objective (D) owing to our own artillery fire, but assisted the others by throwing bombs into the trench.
The enemy being very thick and several men being wounded, 2nd Lieut. Lawrence decided to withdraw his party to the departure ditch. Meanwhile the right party under 2nd Lieut. Lorains had reached their gap in the enemys wire. That Officer and 4 men got on to the parapet, bayoneting a sentry and bombed the trench from the parapet, causing many casualties. They were forced to withdraw owing to superior numbers, but 2nd Lieut. Lorains re-organised in "No Man's Land" and attempted a second attack, which however failed, he himself and several others being wounded in the attempt.
The party then withdrew to the departure ditch and after getting in all the wounded, with the exception of two, one of which was brought in the following night, 2nd Lieut. Lawrence ordered the raiders to withdraw to our trench.
2nd Lieut. Lorains and those of his party who got on to the enemys parapet report that the enemy, who was standing to in Gas Helmets, appeared to be very agitated and disorganised.
Many dead bodies with gas helmets on were seen in the trenches, and it is noteworthy that the raiders never came under Machine gun fire from the portion of the trench attacked, either during the advance or retiring, although occasional burts of machine gun fire were directed on our parapet from our left flank.
None of the patrol experienced any inconvenience from our gas.

CASUALTIES:- Killed, other ranks   1
              Died of wounds, other ranks   2
              Wounded, Officers   2
                 "   other ranks   7
              Missing   "   "   1

The prelininary reconnaissances were carried out by Lieut. R. Cuthbertson, who was wounded while returning from this duty the night of the 28th inst. and was thus unable to command the party which he had organised and trained with great ability. The result proved that his observation of the state of the enemys wire and lie of the ground generally was absolutely correct.

2nd Lieut. E. Lawrence took over the training of the party and carried out the actual operations with great daring and coolness, continuing to direct the operations and assisting in the removal of the wounded, after being wounded himself.

2nd Lieut. J.P. Lorains only joined the party on Lieut. Cuthbertson becoming a casualty. He led his party with great determination and skill, bombing the enemys trench as described above, and endeavoured to make a second assault after the first one had been repulsed, only desisting when he and most of his party were wounded.

The following N.C.O's and men also shewed great gallantry and devotion to duty both in the assault and in bringing in wounded afterwards :-

19612.	Corpl. Gibbs J.G.	Killed while bringing in wounded.
19716.	Pte. Hoyle J.	Bayoneted a sentry, and bombed enemy from parapet. When forced to retire assisted his Officer in organising a seond attack in which he was wounded. Was last man to leave the trench and was killed on way back.
m 7759.	Pte. Walker. J.M.	Killed. Was very conspicuous.
19825.	Pte. Dodds. J.	
16126.	Pte. Jessopp W.	
19695.	Pte. Bruce G.W. (Bruce G.W.)	
19706.	Pte. Danskin J.	
5143M	Pte. Brown A.	
15353M	Sergt. Blythe J.E.	

L/Cpl. Charlton and Ptes. Fulbeck and Collins went out the following night and brought back a missing man.

All the men seem to have shewn great gallantry under very trying circumstances.

In addition to above Capt. E.H. McKerrow R.A.M.C. rendered valuable services in dressing wounded at their arrival at "Dead End".

2/Lt. R.W. Gray, Signalling Officer after conclusion of operations rendered great assistance in bringing in wounded from "No Man's Land".

(Sgd) R.Manners Lt.Col.
Commanding 10th N.F.

1-9-16.

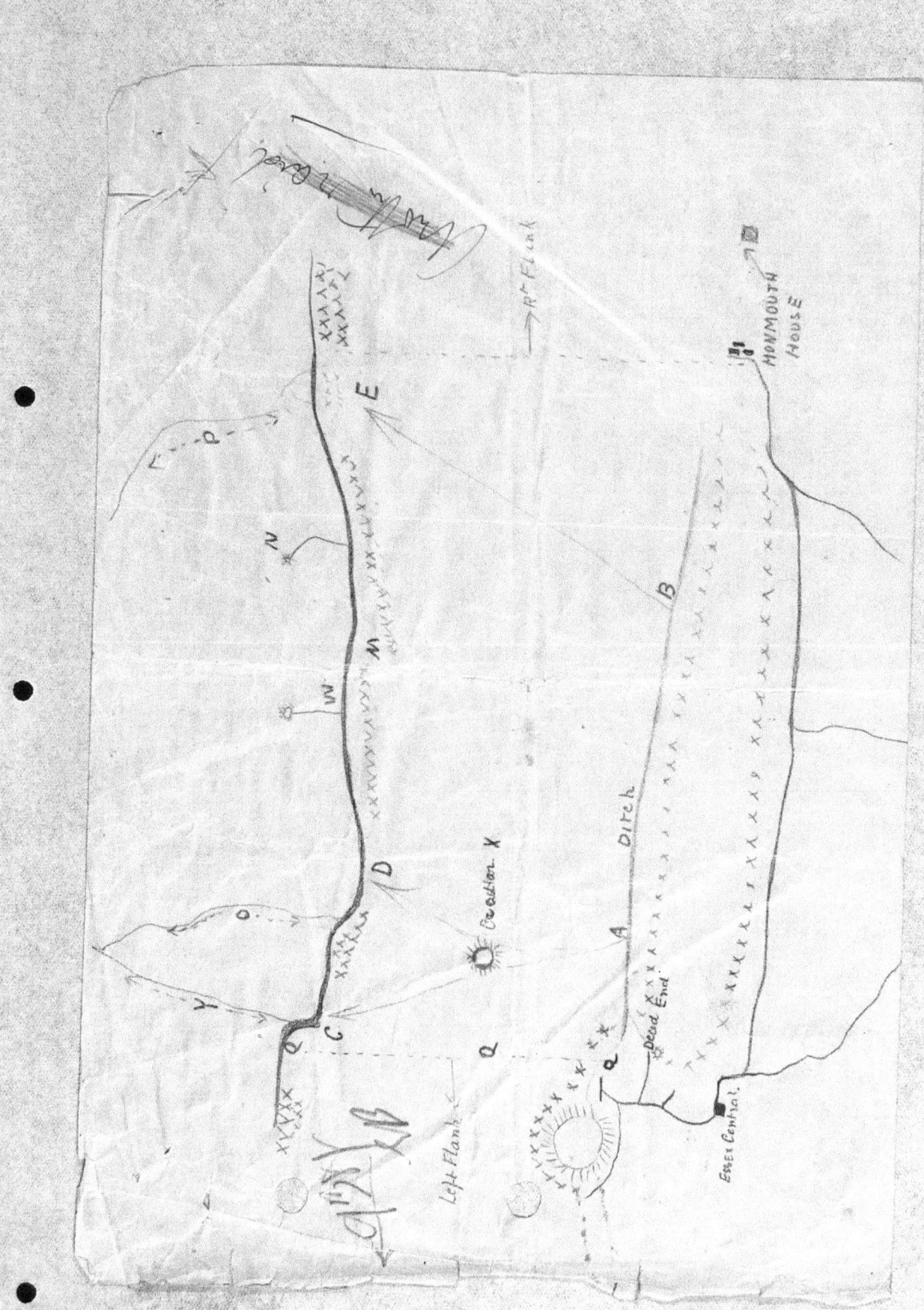

SEPTEMBER

WAR DIARY or INTELLIGENCE SUMMARY.

Army Form C. 2118.

12 N F vol 13

13-e
1916
954f

Place	Date	Hour	Summary of Events and Information	Remarks and references to Appendices
ARMENTIERES	1st		Rain all positions re-arranged. "B" moved 2 platoons to PATERNOSTER ROW - 2 platoons to FUSILIER TERRACE. "C" moved to GD REBECQ. FME.	G.R.
	2nd		Rain. Supplied R.E. working parties.	G.R.
	3rd		Relieved by 4th Gordon Highlanders. Marched to BAILLEUL where we encamped for night of 3/4.	G.R.
BAILLEUL	4th		Marched to billets in COURSE CROIX at 9.45 am. Arrived at 1 pm. Good billets.	G.R.
COURSE CROIX	5th		Moved at 11 am. to BAILLEUR station. Rain outside for ST OMER. Part of 1st line transport travelled by road heading at STAPLES on night train. Arrived ST OMER about 6-15 pm. Wagons & buses at NORTBOULINGHEM. Horses & grooms found on arrival. Men arrived in billets at 9pm. 2Lts LOBB & SUTCLIFFE joined.	G.R.
	6th		Training was carried on between 7.15 am - 1 pm. Closed to heads in RENESCURE, SIQUEVIN, et G. Instruction :	G.R.
	9th		Brigadier-General 61st Infantry Brigade on 7r. 2/Lt CF SAVAGE rejoined en 7r.	G.R.
	10th		Battn marched at 6.30 am to AUDRICQUE entrained then at 9-17. arrived LONGPRE 5pm. Marched to MOLLIENS - AN - BOIS arrived in billets 10.30pm.	G.R.

Army Form C. 2118.

WAR DIARY
or
INTELLIGENCE SUMMARY.
(Erase heading not required.)

Instructions regarding War Diaries and Intelligence Summaries are contained in F.S. Regs., Part II. and the Staff Manual respectively. Title pages will be prepared in manuscript.

Place	Date	Hour	Summary of Events and Information	Remarks and references to Appendices
MOLLIENS AU. BOIS.	11th.		Rain ceases. C.O. inspects billets at 12 noon. Orders received at 4 p.m. for move on the following day.	G.B.
MILLENCOURT	12th.		Marches to MILLENCOURT via BAZIEUX & ACHENCOURT. Arriving in at 1 p.m. Practically the whole of the Bn. was billets. Convention of billets has poor. Major J.H. Llewelyn new rich to C.O.S.	G.B.
"	13th.		Short Coy parades. Inter coy x Soccer Match 1st v 11 N.P. in afternoon.	G.B.
"	14th.		" " " Officers " "	G.B.
"	15th.		Marches from MILLENCOURT at 11 am to BIVOUAC in BECOURT WOOD.	G.B.
BECOURT.	16.		Bn. has part of Coys. reserve & stood by for protection of MM G, G.O.C. Brin for Raiders.	G.B.
"	17		" " " " "	
O.G.1.	18.		Marches at 1.30 p.m. to relieve B.R.s in O.G.1. S. of MARTINPUICH.	G.B.
Men Millencourt			2 Coys. keep O.R. 2 Coy. 6th Avenue. very heavy rain all day. Relief was complete at 4 p.m. L/ Laurence new rich.	
"	19.		Snowy Shows the Ridge by 6th Avenue. Bombed on new C.O.	G.B.
PEAKE WOOD	20.		Bn. Moves back to PEAKE WOOD C. Contamaison.	
"			Casualties 5 O.R. 1 killed & 4 wounded. Officers J.L. DAVIS, A.R. GLEDSTONE. C.F.M. TURNER (minor). Rev. Butler Ret. Ren Rich had evit to Britain.	G.B.

WAR DIARY or INTELLIGENCE SUMMARY

Army Form C. 2118.

Place	Date	Hour	Summary of Events and Information	Remarks and references to Appendices
PEAKE WOOD	21st		Nothing to report.	SF
6C.I.	22nd		Proceeded to "C" position at 4.30 pm taking over trenches for 8th & 9th N.F. Relief completed 7.30 pm. 11th N.F. Coy heavy shells whilst crossing to ridge. Splinters coming through trees.	
		10.20	Cpl. Huffan D.Co.: Wounds Abrasions to L.M. MEDAL. Two killed "	GP
			Lance Cpl. L.C. Rushton of Lawrence's for raid appears to MILITARY CROSS for raid on LE TOUQUET Fr. 20/21 August.	
Bazentin Martinpuich	23rd		Nothing to report.	
Rfords 3 MARTIN POICH	24th.	6.29h	Rain. Move to "B" position relieving the D.S.I. Orders received for attack. Overview to tomorrow day.	GP
	25.		Rain. Attack: details of Operation attached – Relieved by 12 D.S.I. at night. Proceeded to "C" position. Appendix.	GP

WAR DIARY
or
INTELLIGENCE SUMMARY.

(Erase heading not required.)

Army Form C. 2118.

Place	Date	Hour	Summary of Events and Information	Remarks and references to Appendices
Cuinchy	26.	4pm	Relieved by 8th Inds Shropshire Regt. Moved to new position in SCOTTS REDOUBT. Arrived in at 9pm.	GB
SCOTTS REDOUBT	27		Visited by G.O.C. in the morning. C.R.E. Centre in the grounds in the day at 6 p.m.	GB
	28.		Res. heavy. G.O.C. Divn. Cpt arrived to Rein in the afternoon. Instructions on the operations of the Dsk- Suppers.	GB
	29.		Res. heath. working party on Rothuis pair. Carnels of " I.K. B. "	GB
	30		Fine day. " " "	GB

Romsunning
GOC
Cu S9 6 N. F.

ACCOUNT OF ATTACK ON 26TH AVENUE.   25th SEPTEMBER 1916.

24th Sept. The battalion relieved the 12th D.L.I. in "B" position, MARTINPUICH, and received orders to attack 26th AVENUE from POINT 29 on LEFT to POINT 53 on RIGHT, joining up with CANADIAN CORPS at the former point and the 11th N.F. at the latter.
The 12th D.L.I. had endeavoured to carry this length of trench with two platoons earlier in the day, with no success, owing to very heavy Artillery and M.G. fire.
Two Tanks were allotted to the battalion, one to operate from POINT 29 to 26 Central, the other from POINT 53 to 26 Central.

25th Sept. The right tank arrived and took up a concealed position in GUNPIT TRENCH in the early hours of the morning of 25th, the other one got ditched about half a mile to the WEST.

10-0 am. At 10-0 am the Officer i/c of this tank reported to O.C. 16th N.F. that he would not be able to arrive in time to take part in the operations, Zero time having be now been announced as 12-35 p.m. The C.O. therefore telephoned to the Bde Major that he would not attempt to take the trench length POINT 29 - 26 Central.
The Brigadier, however, directed that the attack should take place as originally ordered, with the help of one tank, which should endeavour to work from point 53, along trench to 26 Central, deal with that, then proceed to POINT 29 and move off.
Written orders to this effect were sent to O.C. Tank who asked for 5 minutes start of the Infantry, owing to the difficult nature of the ground.
Two companies were detailed for the attack, "A" on right, "B" on left, with orders not to send over more than two platoons each if these proved successful- but to send all four if necessary..

12-15 pm. Coys were in position, and Tank moving up.
12-21 pm. Tank topped the Rise and became visible to enemy, moving alongside PARK ALLEY towards POINT 53.
12-24 pm. Enemy sent up daylight Rockets.
12-30 pm. Heavy Artillery fire from enemy apparently in response to signals mentioned above.
12-35 pm. Two first lines advanced in perfect order at 50 yards distance in face of very heavy Artillery and Machine Gun fire., those of:-
    "A" 1st Wave under   2nd LIEUT A.S.CALDER.
         2nd " "   2nd LIEUT J.A.LOCK
    "B" 1st " "   LIEUTENANT P.E.JACOBS
         2nd " "   2nd LIEUT H.M.TURNER.
platoons No's 1 & 4 of "A" Coy under the command of 2nd LIEUT NOBLE proceeded in file up PUSH ALLEY.
CAPT CONSTABLE commanding "A" Coy was in this ALLEY directing his Company attack.
The Tank got within about 200 yards of POINT 53, opened fire, moved to the left about 100 yards, then backed down across PUSH ALLEY, out of action

- 2 -

The first wave on topping the rise, which was about 500 yards from our lines and 150 from the enemy suffered very severely, only 2nd LIEUT CALDER, who had been hit on the wrist, and a few men being left to go on.
This party got within 60 yards of the objective., when 2nd LIEUT CALDER was killed, having been hit three times.
2nd LIEUT LOCK brought up No: 3 and remainder of No: 2 platoon, both of which had suffered very heavily.
2nd LIEUT LOCK was struck three times, but struggled on till shot a fourth time, and killed within 150 yards of the objective.
CAPT CONSTABLE then sent orders to 2nd LIEUT NOBLE who was by the disabled Tank in PUSH ALLEY, to extend out over the open and follow the first two waves.
2nd Lieut NOBLE immediately complied but was killed as he got over the parapet.
Seeing that 1 & 4 Platoons could be no good in the open, CAPT CONSTABLE with the assistance of SERT BELL, got the remainder back to the Sap and organized them into Bombing and carrying parties against POINT 53, where they continued at duty till relieved by 12th D.L.I., about 5-15 p.m.
CAPT CONSTABLE then got on the top, apparently to endeavour to organize the remnants of the company. He, however was killed before he had got more than 20 yards.
In the meantime, the attack on the left had fared no better-
LIEUT JACOBS, who led the first wave arrived within about 70 yards of the objective, when, finding he had only a few men with him, he dug in and waited for darkness.
The 3rd and 4th waves under 2nd LIEUT TURNER were severely handled the officer being wounded.
CAPT LINCOLN gave orders to dig in and wait for dark.
With a view to assisting in this, the Commanding Officer ordered Capt ELLIS, Commdg "C" Company to send a platoon to reinforce "B". Capt ELLIS appeared to have personally taken over two platoons and was last seen most gallantly leading them and some of "B" Coy close to the enemy's trench, where he is believed to have been killed.
The attacking parties withdrew under cover of darkness, bringing in the wounded, "D" Coy, which had not been engaged during the day furnishing large parties for this duty, which was ably and courageously carried out under supervision of Capt MC KERROW, R.A.M.C.
The battalion was relieved by the 12th D.L.I. and proceeded to "C" position.

---------------------------------Lieut Colonel.

Commdg 16th (SERVICE) BATTN NORTHUMBERLAND FUSILIERS.

Army Form C. 2118.
VOL 14

WAR DIARY
or
INTELLIGENCE SUMMARY. 18th N.F.
(Erase heading not required.)

Instructions regarding War Diaries and Intelligence Summaries are contained in F. S. Regs., Part II. and the Staff Manual respectively. Title pages will be prepared in manuscript.

Place	Date OCTOBER	Hour	Summary of Events and Information	Remarks and references to Appendices
SCOTS REDOUBT	1st		Reserve position. Working parties to men.	G.B.
"	2nd		" " " " "	
		6 p.m.	Moved to bivouac in Shelter trees as 4 to from Wearsay	G.B.
Shelter trees	3rd	1.30 pm	Continued in new position	
			Moved to "A" position of High Bar relieving 7th N.F. in from of LESARS	G.B.
"A" position		11 pm	Relief complete. A & B. C.C. support line. D.Cy slow line.	
LE SARS.	4th	6 pm	Intense Artillery bombardment of our line. Casualties 5 kills. Wounded –	
		– 8 pm		G.B.
"	5th – 6pm		Intense Artillery bombardment of our line. Chief fire has chicks	
			against Ruffian positions. Casualties 2 killed 1 wounded.	G.B.
	6th –		Relieves by 2 D.L.I. Relief complete midnight.	
"		2 am.	Arrives in Rue d'Elgise line. E. of MARTINPUICH. Casualties 9. Wounded.	G.B.
	7th	1.45 pm	Attack on LE SARS by 68th Bre (12 & 13 D.L.I.). Provide ration parties for attacking Battn. Casualties 4 wounded	G.B. 14–C 1916

#353 Wt. W2544/1454 700,000 5/15 D.D.&L. A.D.S.S./Forms/C. 2118.

Army Form C. 2118.

WAR DIARY
or
INTELLIGENCE SUMMARY.
(Erase heading not required.)

Instructions regarding War Diaries and Intelligence Summaries are contained in F. S. Regs. Part II. and the Staff Manual respectively. Title pages will be prepared in manuscript.

Place	Date Oct 1915	Hour	Summary of Events and Information	Remarks and references to Appendices
Sfondu	8.	2 pm	Relieved by 8th Seaforths (4th Bn. 1st Divn) Arrives to Becourt. Arrives in Becourt 8.30 pm. Casualties 1. Wounded.	G.8.
Becourt	9.		Bn. has baths in Becourt. Road in the afternoon. 2/Lt Murphy arrives.	G.8.
Becourt	10.		1390 L/Sgt Shillock acc. wounded.	G.8.
"	11th. 1pm		Bn. arrives at Albert for Corbie & Longpré. Transport moves by Road.	G.18.
Gorenflos	h.	5.0 pm	Marches from Longpré to Gorenflos. Arrives 4pm.	G.18.
Oneux	13.	4.45 pm	Marches to Oneux = arrives 4-30 pm = 2/Lt Karstel, Murray & Mather arrive	G.18.
"	14.	10 pm	Marches to St Riquier & En Rain entrains for Proven. (Strake Sktn.) 2/Lt Senior, Knox, Uthers, Purington & Co.	G.8.
Laurence Camp.	15.	11 pm	Bn. entrains = moves off at 12.45 am.	G.8.
"	16.	7 am	Arrives at Proven and detrains = marches to Laurence Camp. Poperinghe.	G.8.
"	16.	6.30 pm	Entrains at Laurence Camp for Ypres = Arrives Ypres at 9 pm. Billeted in Ypres Inf. Barracks. Bath J/Sp. Komparts.	G.13.
Ypres	17.		And Coy moves up to Relieve 9 Coy. 28th A.I.F. Cpt a Row Hery. Moves to Station St Ypres.	G.8.

WAR DIARY
or
INTELLIGENCE SUMMARY.
(Erase heading not required.)

Army Form C. 2118.

Place	Date	Hour	Summary of Events and Information	Remarks and references to Appendices
YPRES.	18.	6pm	"C" Coy moves up to the Lion trenches to relieve B. Oz. 9. Reoccupation of "S" portion two Companies "A" Coy moves up to the Inniskillins "B" Baan disposition known =	G.B.
"S" position Trenches	19.		Relieved bed weather. Shell fire no activity on the part of the enemy.	G.B.
	20.		Weather improves. Advance parties of "D.2." arrives previous to the relief by that Baan at night = Relief complete by 8 p.m. & the Baan moves back to huts in the Inf. Reserve YPRES =	G.B.
			Lt. Colthus Rimmer took over Command of the Brigade during the absence on leave of Brig. Genl. Achilles. Capt. Mrs. B. Falks arrives & who accompanies to the Transport lives	G.B.
Dbans YPRES	21.		Remainder no Canadin arrives to Camp here in Lelvers a number two guest Draft 176 have been sent up to YPRES & posted to Coys =	956Y

#353 Wt. W2544/T454 700,000 5/15 D. D. & L. A.D.S.S./Forms/C. 2118.

WAR DIARY or INTELLIGENCE SUMMARY

Army Form C. 2118.

Place	Date	Hour	Summary of Events and Information	Remarks and references to Appendices
"D" Position YPRES.	22.	11 am	C.O. inspects the draft new bases.	G.B.
"	23	7 pm	Relieved by 11th N. Yorks. Regt. entrains 9.30 pm arrives Poperinghe 10 pm. Raw billets in the Railway Depot.	G.B.
Poperinghe	24		3 Coys. pass through the gas hut. Training carries on in accordance with the attacks programme.	G.B.
"	25.	11 am	C.O. inspects the transport line. Lectured on mining at 3 pm.	G.B.
"	26.		Working party of 200 men. Enquiry carried in the fire system of trenches.	G.B.
"	27.		Bac. Rouleau School opened. 2/L Umbers O.C. attends.	G.B.
"	28		Bac. attacks to Roher 3 pm - 5 pm. 300 new bases.	G.B.
"	29		C.O.'s service in the morning 9 am. Review of the Roher bases. Moved to "A" Position relieved 9th Yorks. Relieved at 5 pm. Trains from POPERINGHE to YPRES.	G.B.

Chief Complete to 30 June Quiet night.

Army Form C. 2118.

WAR DIARY
or
INTELLIGENCE SUMMARY.
(Erase heading not required.)

Instructions regarding War Diaries and Intelligence Summaries are contained in F. S. Regs. Part II. and the Staff Manual respectively. Title pages will be prepared in manuscript.

9548
VB

Place	Date	Hour	Summary of Events and Information	Remarks and references to Appendices
Authuille Right Sector	30th	2pm to 11.30 pm	Artillery bombarded enemy trenches opposite the Division on our right. There was slight trench-mortar retaliation on the part of the enemy on its right company, but very little damage was done. Enemy machine guns active on tracks during night.	J.R.B.
	31st	5.30pm	Our heavies fired several rounds at the enemy, in retaliation with trench mortars but no damage was done. Stokes guns shot a dud on our own wire near Lewis gun position at Sap H.	J.R.B.

Geo Rowe Capt a/s
for O.C. 10th Notts &c=

8353 Wt. W3544/1454 700,000 5/15 D. D. & L. A.D.S.S./Forms/C. 2118.

16th NORTHUMBERLAND FUSILIERS.

TRAINING PROGRAMME.

	Oct 24th	25th	26th	27th	28th.
7-15 a.m. to 7-45 a.m.	N I L	PHYSICAL	DRILL	&	BOMBING.
10 a.m. to 11 a.m.	Section & platoon drill	Platoon & Coy. drill	Musketry	Platoon drill	Musketry.
11 a.m. to 12-30 p.m.	BATHG.	ROUTE MARCH.	Coy drill	ROUTE MARCH	Coy drill & Route march.
2 p.m. to 5 p.m.	Arms drill. Lectures to drafts N.C.O.s by O. C. Coys.	Section drill under N.C.O.s	ROUTE MARCH	Coy Drill.	N I L.

REMARKS:- Specialists classes will be formed and will work in accordance with the above working hours.

Classes include - Signalling, Lewis Gunnery, Bombing, and Sniping. Amendments will be made to allow for Gas Lectures etc.

George Rand
Lieut & Adjt

October 22nd. 1916.   For O. C. 16th Northumberland Fusiliers.

Army Form C. 2118.

WAR DIARY
or
INTELLIGENCE SUMMARY.
(Erase heading not required.)

16th Nottl Fusilrs

Vol 15

15 e
1916

Place	Date	Hour	Summary of Events and Information	Remarks and references to Appendices
A position Right Sector trenches	Nov. 1.		Enemy quite mild slight trench-mortaring during the day. Usual machine gun fire on roads at night.	JWD
"	2.		Quiet day. Relieved by 11th NF about 9 p.m. and moved into D position. 2nd Lt B.O.Sullivan proceeded on leave.	JWD
D position Ass Sector YPRES	3.		Working parties. Rifle & gas helmet inspection.	JWD
"	4.		Working parties & fatigues under Coy arrangements.	JWD
"	5.		Working parties & fatigues under Coy arrangements. Voluntary services R.E. C of E & non conformist during morning.	JWD
"	6.		Relieved 11th NF in A position night relief; relief complete 8.30 p.m. Enemy quiet all night	JWD
A position Right Sector trenches	7.		Very wet day causing a great deal of damage to trenches. Very quiet day except for a few shell near DORMY HOUSE about 11 a.m and 1 C Coy retaled for quietly a twelve to Day.	JWD
"	8.		Wet day and very quiet.	JWD
"	9.		Quiet day. Heavily bombarded by enemy trench mortars all along our line from 10.30 p.m to 11.30 p.m.	JWD
"	10.		Relieved by 9th Yorks. Entrained at YPRES & proceeded to ST LAWRENCE CAMP arriving about 11.30 p.m.	JWD

Army Form C. 2118.

WAR DIARY
or
INTELLIGENCE SUMMARY.
(Erase heading not required.)

Instructions regarding War Diaries and Intelligence Summaries are contained in F. S. Regs., Part II. and the Staff Manual respectively. Title pages will be prepared in manuscript.

Place	Date	Hour	Summary of Events and Information	Remarks and references to Appendices
ST. LAWRENCE CAMP	1916 Nov 11.		Coy parades & rededent classes	
"	12.		Last draft inspected by 2/OE Division. Half the batt: innoculated. Church parade R.E. C of E & non Conformists. Remainder of men innoculated.	
"	13.		Coy parades & Specialist classes.	
"	14.		Coy parades & Specialist classes. 2Lt P.G Gibson & Lt W. Smith & 2Lt W.E Blundell reported for duty	
"	15.		Coys commander inspected the Camp 10.0 a.m. Coy parades & rededent classes Major E. Moulton Barrett reported to troop train on arey commander from Capt. Yates.	
"	16.		Batt: moved up to YPRES by train at 5.30 p.m. and relieved 11th Sherwoods in "E" Farm Section left section.	
E Farm left Sector YPRES BARRACKS	17		Working parties & improving billets. Physical training in morning	
"	18		Working parties on billets & for the trenches. Bayonet fighting in morning	
"	19		Church Parade C of E + R.C. Working parties. Lt. Col. Hon Robt: Freeman DSO returned from leave & resumed command of the battalion.	
"	20		Cleaning billets during day. Relieved 11th N.F in A position left Sector about 8.30 p.m.	
A Position Left Sector	21		Relief complete after dusk. Enemy quiet foggy day.	

Army Form C. 2118.

WAR DIARY
or
INTELLIGENCE SUMMARY.
(Erase heading not required.)

Instructions regarding War Diaries and Intelligence Summaries are contained in F. S. Regs., Part II. and the Staff Manual respectively. Title pages will be prepared in manuscript.

Place	Date	Hour	Summary of Events and Information	Remarks and references to Appendices
A Position Left Sector	1916. Nov 22		Enemy quiet all day.	J.S. J.S.
"	23		Enemy quiet all day.	J.S.
"	24		Enemy quiet. Relieved by 11th N.F. & went into "D" position BARRACKS YPRES. Relieve complete at about 9 p.m.	G.B.
"D" position Ypres Barracks	25		Nothing to record.	G.B.
"	26		"	G.B.
"	27		"	
"	28		Move to POPERINGHE. Reserve Battalion of 65th Div. Operation.	G.B
"	29		Move to Lawrence Camp by open train from Ypres-Asnes in hutments at 8.30 p.m.	G.B.
Reserve Lawrence Camp	30		Provide certain fatigue parties. Inter Coy Soccer matches. Hors Debr Rens Jacques, Vinas.	G.B.
"	1		" Training according to attached programme.	G.B.
"	2		"	G.B.

George Nan
Capt. a/s
for Major Cmg.
10 N.F.

WAR DIARY or INTELLIGENCE SUMMARY

Army Form C. 2118.

Vol 7/6 10/N Northumberland Fusiliers

16 c
1915

Place	Date	Hour	Summary of Events and Information	Remarks and references to Appendices
St Omer Camp	DECEMBER 1st		Daily training from 9.30am to 12.30pm and 2pm to 3pm. Following specialist classes formed. Signalling, Lewis Gunnery.	
Corps Reserve Position	7th		Concerts given in Y.M.C.A. Hut on 6th by 6th London Regt & his tenantments. Parties on 5th, 7th respectively. Large audiences on both occasions.	G.S.
			Working parties provided 200 men on 2nd, 70 men on 5th, 5th for work on the front line system. Major H.H. Henery rejoined the Bn from sick leave. 2nd Lt G.H.Q. line reconnoitred on afternoon of 4th by Co. & Senior officers.	
Infts position Right sector	7th		Bn. moves up by train to YPRES to take over "9" position from 9th York & Lancs. Relief complete 9 pm. Major Summerton-Baun. 2nd Lt. Leyh fought 4th + 2.	G.S.
			Relief complete 9 pm. Major Summerton-Baun, 2nd Lt Legh proceeds to take command of 25th M.G.	
" "	8th		Extremely quiet day in trenches. Not the exception of shown T.M.	G.S.
			Bombardment from 2pm – 2.30pm on 8th inst. There were two 01-9u	
Canal Bk	11		Casualties in the trenches. Lieu Gay wounded. "D" Coy.	
ZILLEBEKE BUND.	16		Working parties provided for R.E. Relief postponed from 15th to 16th on account of hostile mis on "9" position. The Bn relieved 11 N Inn.	G.S.
			"9" position commencing at 4 pm. Relief complete 7 pm. Very quiet night. McLachlan & MacKeown... taking fire on 6th. Major Sankom rejoins Battn on 8th.	

Army Form C. 2118.

WAR DIARY
or
INTELLIGENCE SUMMARY.
(Erase heading not required.)

Instructions regarding War Diaries and Intelligence Summaries are contained in F. S. Regs., Part II. and the Staff Manual respectively. Title pages will be prepared in manuscript.

Place	Date	Hour	Summary of Events and Information	Remarks and references to Appendices
"H" Section RIDKIN HOUSE	17		Situation has hormal throughout the 24 hours. Coys have days nights & past trenches in ours after 24 hours in & two parades to have anywhere as at block has been cleared & work of reclaiming commenced.	AB.
	18.		Nothing of importance to report. Camouflet an blown on Hill 60. On account of a sympathetic action from crevices probably has one of our own mine niques deflectors at points were consequently reformed drove cases of an hour or so. Polming however continues. Nil.	GB.
	19. 20.		Enemy artillery has occasionally active throughout the day. OB. blown Sisters blown in in 3 places. Heardocks two clean before relief by n. F. 2. at 7. pm. Cape C.K. hohoma Davie Mb & on Butter two severely wounded by hopen Cokee on his daier between homes as two also his hedical Cpl. Gen Clack+Cp Bot succumbed to their homes at C.C.S. later in the day. Barn moved "45" portin stopie on relief arrising in at about 10 pm.	GB.
"By portin 21. YPRES			Nothing of very much importance happens beyond occasional shelling in	GB.
	23.		YPRES Gurle Close to Our Billets + HQ. VR C, between the Hospice Rive Calledc	

#353 Wt. W2544/1454 700,000 5/15 D. D. & L. A.D.S.S./Forms/C. 2118.

WAR DIARY
INTELLIGENCE SUMMARY

Army Form C. 2118.

Place	Date	Hour	Summary of Events and Information	Remarks and references to Appendices
D position Hopier YPRES:	23.		"D" Coy. Cavalry Barracks: One O.R. rec'd his Carrier on by the Division on our rider & left. Capt McEwen has been at to Coy. at 2 pm on 23rd. 2 party under Major W.R. Hawley. Consisting of 1 offr & Cpl. & 26 O.R. attended Cpl. Clark two buries on the leave day. Our party also attend his funeral service: On Brand 7.30 pm Buses took relieving in "A" position by 11 a.m. Men relief proceeded by 9.30 pm train to Lawrence Camp – arriving in Coy's Reserve as above "f".	Sd.
ST LAWRENCE CAMPS	24.		Nothing of any interest to Cap'tn.	
"	25.		Christmas day: Men off except duty keen. Co. visited leave hut at Brevin three. Their shows have been a failure however both N.O. and Other Ranks to the heavy state of the ground. It has to be cancelled. The Whitsun M.P. Batt. M.P. gave a concert in Hut R. this from 5.30pm to 7.3. for which our much enjoys.	G.R.

WAR DIARY
or
INTELLIGENCE SUMMARY.

(Erase heading not required.)

Army Form C. 2118.

Place	Date	Hour	Summary of Events and Information	Remarks and references to Appendices
Coppestein ST LOUIS R.G.E. Camp G.H.E.	26th		Parade daily for Arti marching etc. Signalling R.G. Classes formed. 1/smm on working party on front system of trenches on each day on 24th.	G.R.
	31st		175 men on new supplies. Rations at 4.30 pm on 31st late owing to "M" position left later from 912. Relief complete 8.30 pm. Quiet night. Working 6 repair.	G.R. Cas.B.

Malton Major.
Commanding 1st Bn North S.

31.12.16

2353 Wt. W2544/1454 700,000 5/15 D. D. & L. A.D.S.S./Forms/C. 2118.

10th North Stus Oct 1917

Jonny —

SUBJECT.

No.	Contents.	Date.
	General Edmonds. Index to Correspondence File.	

WAR DIARY
or
INTELLIGENCE SUMMARY.

Army Form C. 2118.

10 NF
8 of 17

Place	Date JANUARY	Hour 1917	Summary of Events and Information	Remarks and references to Appendices
"A" position LEFT SECTOR HOTOILLERET	1.		Quiet morning. Artillery & T.M. activity on our front. Kensington Avenue being subjected to heavy fire. Capt. Hon. B. Bulter has promised to assist also b men. Retaliation has asked for and our guns replied effectively. Quiet night.	G.B.
"	2		There was desultor activity as on the previous day & some damage has done to our front line trenches. Quiet morning. No snipers	G.B.
"	3.		Nothing to report. Except slight shelling of our front.	G.B.
"	4.		Quietest day of the tour. he new relieves by "N.Z. arty. Bom. & previous to "C." position. Ypres Inf. Barracks. were to A. Bogen. "B" occupies a position in WELLINGTON CRESCENT. When "C." position.	G.B.
"C" position Inf Barrack	5.		He men were employed on working parties. There was shells in & 8 S.G. or 4.2 throughout the day. Barracks & Catherine hen hit several times. There were Cpl. Coomalis in Off. Refs in the Shack	G.B.
	8.			G.B.½

Army Form C. 2118.

WAR DIARY
or
INTELLIGENCE SUMMARY.
(Erase heading not required.)

Instructions regarding War Diaries and Intelligence Summaries are contained in F. S. Regs., Part II. and the Staff Manual respectively. Title pages will be prepared in manuscript.

Place	Date	Hour	Summary of Events and Information	Remarks and references to Appendices
"A" Bastion LARK'S ECTOR	8	4.30 pm	Commenced relief of "A" N.B.	GA
		7.30	Relief complete. Quiet night. Co. visited the lines from	
		10 pm – 1.30 am.		
"	9.		Slight hostile artillery activity on support position. RITZ St into Shelled between 4.45 pm & 5.15 pm. Cpl. Sleep taken wounded.	GA
"	10.		Nothing unusual to report. A few S.O.S. were sent over by lamp – not very successful.	GA
"	11.		Quiet day.	
"D" Bastion	12.		Quiet day. Relieved by 11 M.I. at 7.30 pm. Moves to "D" Bastion INF. Barracks.	GA
INF. BARRACKS	12/16		Nothing to report. R.E. working parties from Bastion. Moved into Coys. Reserve at Lawrence Camp by 7.30 pm. Train from YPRES.	GA
LAWRENCE CAMP	17			GA
	2		Training in accordance with programme attached. Owing to services being carried out in conjunction with R.F.E. a orders have been modified with 1/2 the unit & signal etc.	GA

Army Form C. 2118.

WAR DIARY
or
INTELLIGENCE SUMMARY.
(Erase heading not required.)

Instructions regarding War Diaries and Intelligence Summaries are contained in F.S. Regs., Part II. and the Staff Manual respectively. Title pages will be prepared in manuscript.

Place	Date	Hour	Summary of Events and Information	Remarks and references to Appendices
Shrewsbury Camp.	24th	3.45pm	Parades for trenches & entrained at 5.45 p.m. Rain very heavy.	GR
"B" Bank Right Sector			Relieves 8th K.O.Y.L.I. in "B" position. Relief complete at midnight. Thrown away canvas by strips. Slates of the ducks boards.	
	25.		Continuous heavy fire. Wire emergency reported broken on the L.S.I.	
	26.		The town was a very quiet one, there being only H Coaracaine. One of which was caused by our own artillery, which on the 27th was firing short. Caused no damage to very few breastworks.	GR
			Rain has ceased. O "N.S. at 8. Pinion 27th -	
			Proceeded to "C" position in Bee Reserve.	
	28.		Prisoners "C" position by Q. So. Bn. - 3. Corp (ABC) & Bn. of In'to Bond. "D" Coy STAFFORD Bzn.	GR
"Caesars"	29th		Nothing unusual occurred: there was a little shelling of the actual	GR
Camp.	30.		Bund O'the Allungut of B.W. but no damage was done. Air priorities.	GR

[signature] Major
Comdg. 13th Bn.

10th BATTALION NORTHUMBERLAND FUSILIERS.

TRAINING PROGRAMME.

17th TO 24th JANUARY, 1917.

HOURS.	17th.	18th.	19th.	20th.	21st.	22nd.	23rd.	24th.
7-15 a.m. to 7-45 a.m.	Cleaning up.	Physical Drill and Doubling.	Bayonet Fighting.	Physical Drill.	NIL.	BAYONET FIGHTING.	Physical Drill and Doubling	
10-0 a.m. to 11-0 a.m.	Arms Drill.	Route March. Platoon Drill.	Bathing. Route March.	Company Drill.	CHURCH	Musketry. Platoon Drill. Kit Inspect.	Coy. Drill Bathing.	
11 a.m. to 12-30 p.m.	Platoon Drill.	Route March. Company Drill.	Bathing. Route March.	Company Drill.	PARADE.	Kit Inspect. Coy. Drill.	Bathing. Kit Inspect. Coy. Drill.	Cleaning up.
1-45 p.m. to 3-0 p.m.	Company Drill. Lecture by M.O. on First Aid.	Musketry. Lecture by M.O. on First Aid.	Lecture by M.O. on First Aid.	NIL.	NIL.	Lecture by M.O. on First Aid. Section Drill. Communication Drill.	First Aid. Section Drill. Communication Drill.	NIL.

SPECIALISTS = SIGNALLERS CLASS.
LEWIS GUNNERS.-- (PROGRAMME OF WORK ATTACHED).

George Dumb apirap
for Major.
Commanding 10th Battalion Northumberland Fusiliers.

16th January, 1917.

Army Form C. 2118.

WAR DIARY
or
INTELLIGENCE SUMMARY.
(Erase heading not required.)

10 N F

Vol 18

Instructions regarding War Diaries and Intelligence Summaries are contained in F. S. Regs., Part II. and the Staff Manual respectively. Title pages will be prepared in manuscript.

Place	Date	Hour	Summary of Events and Information	Remarks and references to Appendices
"C" position BUND	FEBRUARY 1917 1st		The day was quiet.	16 e
		5 pm	Relief of 11th N.F. in "B" position commenced from the Bund.	G.O.A.
		9 pm	Relief was complete. Coys are disposed as follows. B. C. D. front Coys from right to left. "A" Coy in support. Bn H.Q. DORMY H.O.	
"D" position R.I. SECTOR	2nd		Quiet night. Trenches were dry C left up one to four look outs. Hipades by snow fall. "C" Coy has stakes during the morning. The holes being bounded.	G.O.
"	3rd		Nothing of Importance to record.	G.O.
"	4th		~ ditto ~	
"	5th:		Quiet day. H. 4. 30 Bn. Bann H.Q. moves from DORMY H⁰ to VALLEY COTTAGES, handing over to 11 N.F. to incoming unit at the latter place. Bann was relieved by 9.30 pm & proceeded to "D" position = Bann Airfires at Johan. H.Q. B & C. The Bund. "D" Riding Gate & YPRES "D" KRUISSTRAAT=	G.O.
"D" position BUND.				

WAR DIARY
or
INTELLIGENCE SUMMARY.
(Erase heading not required.)

Army Form C. 2118.

Place	Date	Hour	Summary of Events and Information	Remarks and references to Appendices
"D" position BUND.	5.		Lt Col Lord Brassey CMG D.S.O. rejoined Bn after one months leave to	Gd.
	6.7.8.		ENGLAND. NIL Parties basis her parties for R.E.	Gd. App.
	9.	10pm	Relieved by 9th Yorks Regt & proceed to Corps Reserve.	Gd. C.
Skinners Camp.	10.	12.30am	Bn has arrived in the Camp.	Gd.
"	11	10.30am	Church Parade: Hon. Chaplain General & Army Brigadier G.O.C. Division attended the Service.	Gd.
"		6pm	Lecture by the Adjutant on "the platoon as an offensive unit"	Gd.
	12.		G.O.C. Division has done the Comp. His reorganisation of platoon	Gd.
	13.		Commenced: women unloading bivvy of ABEELE.	
"	14.		Training in accordance with Armies programme.	
"	15.		"	Gd.

WAR DIARY
or
INTELLIGENCE SUMMARY.
(Erase heading not required.)

Army Form C. 2118.

Place	Date	Hour	Summary of Events and Information	Remarks and references to Appendices
Shamma Camp	16.	11.15	Brigadier General G.St. Rue inspects the lines.	G.d.
	17.	2.15pm	Russian Guard for promulgation of S.G.Co.M.	G.d.
			Young = lees how Rhamin Cua. S's admitted to hospital with Influenza. 2Lt S.J. 4 Umber to hospital. Temperature 103°. JASTON M.C. Commands "A"Coy.	
		6pm	Russian Guards hair 3 hour Silence	A.D.P.
R. Pm.			9th Yor. Regt. in "B" Section left Sector relief complete	G.d.
LEFT SECTOR	18.		2.Swn = Quiet day. "A" & "B" from line Coy. R. Support. "C" Reserves. 2Lt L.N. WILKINSON reports for duty. attaches to "A" Coy.	G.d.
	19.	4.20	HALFWAY St: Ans Brew H.Q. hrs. subjected to heavy bombardment.	G.d.
			for 20 minutes. 2New "C" Coy (Cooks) wounded. 19730 Pte RENWICK.T.	
			6256. GRAHAM. J.S. 6189. Pte. Rn. CARVER.	
"	20		Raid by Division on our STque (47) was carried on at 5pm.	X
			Own line were subjected to slight retaliation.	
"	21		Rear S.O.S. was sent up at 6pm from "D"Coy in BOND St. On account	O.f.p.
"	22.		of the fog this was u/s/d	X.E.
			Relieved by 4 N.F. Relief complete 7. Bopm Yorkshires to the position INF. Barracks	

Army Form C. 2118.

WAR DIARY
or
INTELLIGENCE SUMMARY.
(Erase heading not required.)

Instructions regarding War Diaries and Intelligence Summaries are contained in F. S. Regs., Part II. and the Staff Manual respectively. Title pages will be prepared in manuscript.

Place	Date	Hour	Summary of Events and Information	Remarks and references to Appendices
"C"	22.		Bn. arrive at 6 p.m.	St.
Position Left Sector Inf. Barr.	23rd		Nothing unusual occurred. R.E. Batric. Supplies. 2/Lt. A.B. FERGUSON joined Bn. on 23rd.	
	24th		Relieving Battn. form 17th. The Camp up on 25th.	St. app.
	25.		Relieved by 17th. K.R.R.C. at 7 p.m. & proceeds to POPERINGHE by train leaving YPRES. 9.15 p.m. Marches from POPERINGHE	St. -F.
	26.		to "G" Camp. Arrive in "G" Camp. 11 p.m.	
"G" Camp	27.		Rested & cleans up. Lt. Col. hon R. Monners C.M.G. D.S.O. rejoins Baralion. 6th Affiliated 10th Bn. attached to Baron for the move.	St. G.
			Bn. marches from "G" Camp at 9 a.m. to SOOTRERVE	
SOOTRERVE	28.		Arriving in SOOTRERVE at 12.30 p.m. Rested in the afternoon distance of march 9/10 miles.	G Z

LCStovell
CmD. 10th N.F.

SECRET.   COPY NO. 9

BATTALION OPERATION ORDER NO. 100

1. Battalion will relieve the 11th Battalion Northumberland Fusiliers in "B" position Right Sector to-morrow, 1st February.

2. The Battalion will be disposed as follows :-

    Right Company.   "B"
    Centre Company.   "C"
    Left Company.   "D"
    Support Company. "A"

    Battalion Headquarters.   DORMY HOUSE.

3. The relief will commence from the BUND at 5-0 p.m. Companies will pass the starting point, Battalion Headquarters, as follows :-

    Headquarters.   - 5-0 p.m.
    "C" Company.   - 5-5 p.m.
    "B" Company.   - 5-11 p.m.
    "D" Company.   - 5-18 p.m.
    "A" Company.   - 5-24 p.m.

    Route via South edge of the BUND.

4. All Trench Stores, Defence Schemes, Secret Maps, Log-books, and Air Photos, will be taken over and lists forwarded to Battalion Headquarters by 7-0 a.m. on the 2nd prox.

5. Advance parties will proceed to trenches at 11-30 a.m. to-morrow.

6. Baggage, blankets, stores etc for return to the Quartermaster Stores and conveyance to the lines, will be stacked at the South West corner of the BUND at 4-30 p.m. Small loading parties will be detailed by Company Commanders.

7. "A", "B" and "C" Companies will draw 50 pair of Gumboots each, Headquarters 10 pairs, from the G.S.D.R. the BARRACKS between 11-0 a.m. and 1-0 p.m. to-morrow. Equal distribution of Gumboots will be arranged between O. C. Companies in the line.

8. Two lorries will convey blankets to the Q.M.Stores.

9. Disposition reports will be rendered to Battalion Headquarters by 7-0 a.m. on the 2nd prox.

10. 2nd Lt. J. L. Davis will be attached to "C" Company. 2nd Lt. W. M. Bowler to "D" Company for this tour.

11. Completion of reliefs will be reported to Battalion Headquarters.

12. ACKNOWLEDGE.

[signature]
Captain and Adjutant.
10th Battalion Northumberland Fusiliers.

Copy No. 1. "A" Company.
"   " 2. "B" Company.
"   " 3. "C" Company.
"   " 4. "D" Company.
"   " 5. T.O.
"   " 6. O.M.
"   " 7. M.O.
"   " 8. O.D.
"   " 9. Office.

B

SECRET.   COPY No.

19th BATTALION NORTHUMBERLAND FUSILIERS OPERATION ORDER No. 101.

Reference Map KILLBEEK.
28 N.W. 4. & N.E.5 1/10,000

1. The Battalion will be relieved by the 11th Battalion Northumberland Fusiliers in "D" position to-morrow night, 6th February, and on relief will withdraw into Divisional Reserve "D" position, taking over from the 13th D. L. I.

2. The Battalion will be disposed as follows:-

    "B" Company. }
    "C" Company. }   -   ZILLEBEKE BUND

    "A" Company.   -   RIDING SCHOOL.

    "D" COMPANY.   -   KRUISSTRAAT.

    Battalion Headquarters. - KILLEBEKE BUND.

3. All trench stores, defence schemes, secret maps and log-books, will be handed over to the incoming Unit in "D" position, and taken over from outgoing Unit in "D" position, lists of which will be forwarded to Battalion Headquarters by 9-0 a.m. on 6th inst.

4. No trench or portion of trench will be vacated until occupied by 11th Northumberland Fusiliers.

5. Baggage, stores etc, for conveyance to "D" position will be stacked at the Ration Dump KILLEBEKE, after dusk. On no account must there be any movement before 5-15 p.m. Two men per Company will be told off to accompany the wagon which will stop at Transport Farm, Riding School and Kruisstraat.

6. The Transport Officer will arrange for transport to be at KILLEBEKE Ration Dump, as early as possible to convey baggage etc, to "D" positions. Allotment as follows :-

    Headquarters.   - Mess Cart.
    Orderly Room and Signal Stores. - 1. L. G. S. Wagon.
    4 Companies.   - 1 L. G. S. Wagon.
    M. O. Maltese Cart.

7. Advance parties will leave trenches at 1-30 p.m. to take over new position. 2nd Lt. N. M. Fowler will supervise taking over.

8. Quartermaster will arrange for rations to be sent up by 1st line transport to-morrow night.

9. Two lorries will bring up the blankets.

10. All Gumboots will be taken out of the line and returned to O.F.D.S. on morning of the 6th inst.

11. Completion of relief will be reported to Battalion Headquarters by an Officer of each Company on his way out and completion of moves and dispositions report by runner on arrival in.

12. ACKNOWLEDGE.

                                            George Bunel.
                                        ....
                                         Captain and Adjutant.
                                    19th Battalion Northumberland Fusiliers.

Copy. No. 1. "A" Company.   Copy No. 2. "B" Company.

Copy No. 3. - O. C.
"   " 4. - "B" Company.
"   " 5. - "C"   "
"   " 6. - H. Q.
"   " 7. - 2. i/c
"   " 8. - 2nd in Command.
"   " 9. - Office.

SECRET.   **COPY NO.**

10th BATTALION NORTHUMBERLAND FUSILIERS. OPERATION ORDER NO. 102.

1. The Battalion will be relieved in "D" position, Right Sector, by the 9th Battalion Yorks Regiment to-morrow, 9th February.

2. <u>On relief</u> the Battalion will withdraw into Corps Reserve at ST LAWRENCE CAMP.

3. The Battalion will entrain at YPRES SIDING.

4. H. Q. and Companies will move to the place of entrainment via shortest routes.

5. Formation - platoons at 100 yards interval.

6. All guards, control posts, stores etc, will be handed over and receipts for same, together with billet clean certificates, forwarded to Orderly Room by 10-0 a.m. on the 10th inst.

7. 2nd Lt. F. C. BLUNDELL will proceed in advance of the Battalion to YPRES SIDING, and acquaint himself with the exact point of entrainment.

8. Transport Officer will arrange for the following transport to be at the disposal of H. Q. and Companies.:-

    H. Q.   1. L. G. S. Wagon and Mess Cart.

    Each Company. 1. L. G. S. Wagon.

9. Baggage, blankets etc, will be stacked at following points between 5-30 p.m. and 6-30 p.m. :-

    H. Q. "B" and "C"   -   Transport Farm.

    "A" and "D".   -   Company. H. Q.

10. 1 Lorry will convey Battalion blankets. A guide will be detailed from H. Q. to conduct lorry to "A" and "D" Companies Headquarters. Lorry will be at Transport Farm at 6-0 p.m.

11. Advance Parties of N. C. O's per H. Q. and Companies will parade under 2nd Lt. J. C. Ray at "B" Company's Headquarters, KRUISSTRAAT at 10-0 a.m. and will proceed to ST LAWRENCE CAMP to take over.

12. ACKNOWLEDGE.

George Bewsh
Captain and Adjutant.
10th Battalion Northumberland Fusiliers.

8th February. 1917. Copy No 1. "A" Company.   Copy No. 2. "B" Company.   Copy No. 3. "C".
         "   " 4. "D" Company.   "   " 5. T. O.   "   " 6. Q. M.
         "   " 7. C. O.   "   " 8. O. Office.   "   " 9.

SECRET.   COPY NO. 9.

10th BATTALION NORTHUMBERLAND FUSILIERS. OPERATION ORDER NO. 103.

1. The Battalion will relieve 9th Battalion York and Lancs in "B" position Left Sector, to-morrow night, February. 17th.

2. Dispositions will be as follows :-

    Battalion Headquarters.   -   HALFWAY HOUSE.

    Right Company.
    "D" Company.   2 Platoons.   Trench I. 18. 4 and 5.
                    2   "   "   ROSSLYN STREET.
    Company Headquarters.   -   BOND STREET LOCALITY.

    Left Company.
    "A" Company.   2 Platoons.   Trench I. 17. 1 and 2.
                    1 Platoon.   Trench.I. 17. 4.
                    1 Platoon.   THE CULVERT.
    Company Headquarters.   -   BIRR. CROSS. ROADS.

    Support Company.
    "B" Company.   1 Platoon.   ROSSLYN STREET.
                    3 Platoons.   OXFORD STREET and LEINSTER SREET.
    Company Headquarters.   -   LEINSTER STREET.

    Reserve Company.
    "C" Company.   3 Platoons.   HALFWAY HOUSE.
                    1 Platoon.   RAILWAY CUTTING. (I. 16. a. "5. 8.)
    Company Headquarters.   -   HALFWAY HOUSE.

    Regimental Aid Post.   -   HALFWAY HOUSE.

3. The Battalion will parade at 6-0 p.m. and march to level crossing, G. 11. C. 0. 9. in the following order :-

    Headquarters.   "A"., "D"., "B"., "C".

    and will entrain at 6-45 p.m.   Guides will be at LILLE GATE.

4. Trench Stores, log-books, defence schemes, maps and air photos' will be taken over, and lists of the same forwarded to Battalion Headquarters by 10-0 a.m. on the 18th inst.

5. Officers' baggage, blankets, stores etc, for conveyance to the trenches and Q. M. Stores, will be stacked outside Orderly Room and Guard Room respectively by 4-30 p.m.   Small loading parties will be detailed by Company Commanders.

6. The Transport Officer will arrange for the following transport for conveyance of Trench baggage :-

    Battalion Headquarters.   -   Mess Cart and 1 L. G. S. Wagon.
    Companies.   -   1 L. G. S. Wagon each.
    M. O.   -   Maltese Cart.

7. Gumboots will be drawn from Guard Room at 12-30 p.m.

8. Advance parties as follows will parade outside Orderly Room at 9-30 a.m.

    Headquarters.   -   2 N. C. O's
    Companies.   -   1 Officer and 1 N. C. O. Each.
    Battalion Signalling N. C. O. and 2 O. R.
    Battalion Bombing N. C. O.
    Battalion Lewis Gun Officer and 1 N. C. O.
    No bus is available.

9. 2nd Lt. J. L. Umbers will act as L. G. O. for this tour.

10th. Brigade Observers will report to Sgt. Lockey. 12th D. L. I. at MONTREAL CAMP at 9-30 a.m.

11. Completion of relief will be reported to Battalion Headquarters and dispositions rendered by 12 midnight.

12. ACKNOWLEDGE.

George Hand
Captain and Adjutant.

16th February, 1917.

Copy No. 1. "A" Company.
" " 2. "B" "
" " 3. "C" "
" " 4. "D" "
" " 5. T. O.
" " 6. Q. M.
" " 7. C. O.
" " 8.
" " 9. Office.

SECRET.   COPY No. 9

10th BATTALION THE NORTHUMBERLAND FUSILIERS.

OPERATION ORDER No. 104.

1. The Battalion will be relieved in "B" position by 11th Battalion Northumberland Fusiliers, to-morrow night, 22nd February.

2. On relief the Battalion will withdraw to "C" position INFANTRY BARRACKS, YPRES. (Brigade Reserve) taking over billets from 11th Battalion Northumberland Fusiliers. Defence schemes etc, from 15th Durham Light Infantry.

3. Headquarters and Companies will occupy billets as on previous occasions.

4. All trench stores, log-books and secret maps will be handed over to the relieving Unit. Lists of same will be forwarded to Battalion Headquarters by 9-0 a.m. 23rd inst.

5. All gumboots will be taken out of the line and handed into the G. B. D. R. BARRACKS before 12-0 noon on the 23rd inst.

6. Wagons will report at the Transport Lines to-morrow to convey Battalion's blankets to "C" position.

7. Baggage, stores etc, will be stacked at the Ration Dump at 6-0 p.m. 2 men per Company will remain as loading party and will accompany the wagons.

8. The Transport Officer will arrange for the following Transport to be at the disposal of Headquarters and Companies for purpose stated in paragraph 7. :-

    Headquarters.   -   Mess Cart and 1 L. G. S. Wagon.

    4 Companies.   -   1 L. G. S. Wagon.

    M. O.   -   Maltese Cart.

9. Advance parties of 2 N. C. O's per Company and Headquarters will report to 2nd Lt. J. MURPHY at the Headquarters. 11th Battalion Northumberland Fusiliers. BARRACKS at 2-30 p.m.

10. Reliefs will be reported to Battalion Headquarters by an Officer of each Company on his way out, and completion of moves by runner.

11. ACKNOWLEDGE.

                                    George Sand
                                    Captain and Adjutant.
                                    10th Battalion Northumberland Fusiliers.

Copy No. 1. "A" Company.   Copy No. 4. "D" Company.   Copy No. 7. L.G.O.
"   " 2. "B" Company.   "   " 5. T. O.   "   " 8. C. O.
"   " 3. "C" Company.   "   " 6. Q. M.   "   " 9. Office.

21st February. 1917.

F.

War Diary

SECRET.   COPY NO. 9

10TH BATTALION. THE NORTHUMBERLAND FUSILIERS.
OPERATION ORDER No. 105.

1. The Battalion will be relieved in "C" position, Left Sector by 17th Battalion K. R. R. C. on night of 26th February, 1917.

2. On relief, the Battalion will proceed to Camp "G". A. 16. b. 2. 5. by train to POPERINGHE, leaving YPRES at 8-30 p.m.

3. The Battalion will parade in the Colonnade at 7-45 p.m. and will march to the Siding in the order - H. Q., "D", "B", "C", "A", Companies. Formation. - 50 yards distance between platoons.

4. Billet stores will be handed over to the incoming Unit and receipts forwarded to this Office by 9-30 a.m. on 24th inst.

5. Officers Kit, Blankets, Stores etc. for removal to new position, will be stacked by the Battalion Guardroom by 4-0 p.m. on the 26th. Small loading parties will remain to load up and to travel with same to Camp "G".

6. Advance parties of N. C. O's per Company and Headquarters under 2nd Lt. L. A. GIBSON will parade at Orderly Room at 9-0 a.m. on 26th inst and will proceed by march route to Camp "G" to take over. One guide per Company and Headquarters will meet the battalion at POPERINGHE STATION.

7. 2nd Lt. E. S. Brown and guides at the rate of 1 per Company and Headquarters will be detailed to meet the incoming Unit at BRIDGE 10, RAILWAY CROSSING at 8-30 p.m. They will report to 2nd Lt. A. S. Brown at Orderly Room at 8-0 p.m.

8. From the 27th inst (inclusive) the 23rd Division will be administered by VIII Corps.

9. ACKNOWLEDGE.

George Lund.
Captain and Adjutant.
10th Battalion Northumberland Fusiliers.

```
Copy No. 1.  "A" Company.
  "    "   2.  "B"    "
  "    "   3.  "C"    "
  "    "   4.  "D"    "
  "    "   5.  T. O.
  "    "   6.  O. C.
  "    "   7.  Adjt.
  "    "   8.  L. G. O.
  "    "   9.  War Diary.
```

24th February, 1917.

SECRET   COPY No. 9

10th BATTALION NORTHUMBERLAND FUSILIERS.

OPERATION ORDER No. 106.

1. The Battalion will leave "C" Camp to-morrow, and proceed by march route to HOUTKERQUE, AREA.

2. ROUTE - POPERINGHE - ST JAN - ter - BIEZEN. 2nd Lt. E. Wrighton will be responsible for the direction.
Order of march - H. Q. "A", "B", Band, "C"., "D"., L. G. Handcarts. Transport.

3. The Battalion will parade on the PARADE GROUND at 9-45 a.m. facing S. E.

4. The 1st Line Transport will be drawn up in the lines L. & A. ready to move in rear of the column at 10-15 a.m. Officers chargers will be sent to "D" Camp.

5. Officers' valises, blankets stores etc, will be stacked at Q. M. Stores by 8-0 a.m. to-morrow. 6 men per Company and Headquarters will be detailed as loading party and guard over same.

6. Steel Helmets, Leather jerkins and Box Respirators will be stacked at Q. M. store at 8-30 p.m. to-day. Leather jerkins and Box respirators will be tied into Section bundles. It is essential that all these articles are clearly marked with owner's No's. Rank, name, platoon and Company, and that the packing in the lorry is as compact as possible. Loading parties will be detailed.

7. Attached details of officer and Other Ranks will march as a Company in rear of "D" Company.

8. ACKNOWLEDGE.

George Bend
Captain and Adjutant.
10th Battalion Northumberland Fusiliers.

Copy No 1. "A" Company.
"   " 2. "B" Company.
"   " 3. "C" Company.
"   " 4. "D" Company.
"   " 5. T. O.
"   " 6. Q. M.
"   " 7. L. G. O.
"   " 8. O. O.
"   " 9. War Diary.

10 N F
Vol 19

Army Form C. 2118.

WAR DIARY
or
INTELLIGENCE SUMMARY.
(Erase heading not required.)

Place	Date MARCH	Hour	Summary of Events and Information	Remarks and references to Appendices
HOUTKERQUE MILLAIN	1st	9am	Battalion Marches from MILLAIN to HOUTKERQUE. Distance about 19 miles in accordance with Brigade Operation Order No 107. The marching was satisfactory. Only 3 men fell out of the column. Excellent weather.	App. A. G.R.
MILLAIN	2		Day spent in Cleaning up. Officers reconnoitres area of training area	G.R.
"	3.		Coy parades. re-organisation. Steady drill. "A" Coy on the range. G.O.C. Division visited "C" Coy at work in the training area in the afternoon. afterwards broke our ramparts. Church parades. Lt. P. Sinn. reported for duty. Lt. A. Mayer Jo'd II Army Signal Sch. D. arrival. Afternoon devoted to recreation.	G.R. G.R.
"	4.		Coy parades "B" Coy on the range. (A.27.6.) = Major General Cuth. Bee visited Companies during the morning.	G.R.
"	5.		Coy parades. Co. learned to Spears operation. Superints on training.	G.S.
"	6.		Coy parades "C" Coy on the ranges. Co. learned to Spears operation. Sings or	G.S.
"	7.		training Coy parades. Tactical exercise carried on in the afternoon. Sting	G.R.
"	8.		of travens Coy parades "D" Coy on the range. O.C. "B" Coy. A.Sgn. Burnie. Maujor. ↓ R. M. Etap	G.R.
"	9.		at the ROOLEZEELE Ranges	G.R.
"	10.		"A" & "B" Coys Abotes training area. "C" & "D" Coys Running. Cross-Country Runs in the afternoon	G.R.

1917

Army Form C. 2118.

WAR DIARY
or
INTELLIGENCE SUMMARY.
(Erase heading not required.)

Place	Date	Hour	Summary of Events and Information	Remarks and references to Appendices
MILLAIN	MARCH		Note.	
	11th		Up to the 10th training was for the most part devoted to Sectional back-	
			Church Parade. Tactical Exercise for officers in the morning	G.R.
"	12.	2.15	Signallers & proportion of officers attended Contact Patrol Exercise on Oving	G.R
			to Wizernes. The exercise has concluded on the grounds. 2/Lt. F.C. WHYTE	
			joined for duty & taken on the strength	
"	13.		"C" & "D" Companies on the training Area.	G.R
"	14.		Lewis Gunners fired on the range A, B, 6. Companies - Peleven training	
"	15.		" B " Training trop. "C" & D companies peleton training	G.R
"	16.17		" D " Peleton training. A & B companies 2/Lt reports sick reports No duty no annual -	
			" D " Baths. Attack Exercise was carried out - In the morning - afternoon -	
"	18		Foot inspection.	
"			Church Parade. Bathing & preparation for march.	G.R.
HERZEELE	19.		Moved to HERZEELE at 9.5 am arrived HERZEELE 2. 30 p.m. Route Sca8acca	G.R
			Over large area.	
	20		Left HERZEELE 10.10 am. arrived "Y" camp. 12.15 p.m.	G.R
Y Camp.	21.		Left Y. Camp. at 9.30 am moved by march route to "D" Camp arriving thus at 12.5 p.m.	G.R
Infantry Brigadier "D" Camp	22.		Supplied working party of 250 men for Burnie Cake System: hours of work 9 am — 2pm G.R	

Army Form C. 2118.

WAR DIARY
or
INTELLIGENCE SUMMARY.
(Erase heading not required.)

Instructions regarding War Diaries and Intelligence Summaries are contained in F.S. Regs., Part II. and the Staff Manual respectively. Title pages will be prepared in manuscript.

Place	Date	Hour	Summary of Events and Information	Remarks and references to Appendices
"D" Camp. A.30.A. Sheet 28N.W.	MARCH 23rd		Coy parade. Platoon training. Range practice. following Officers posted to Bttn. reported for duty 2/Lieuts. B. HALON, T.L. ANDERSON, P.L. DELANY, H.F.N. KNOWLES, R.A. DENT, W. SWINDELL.	G.R.
	24th		C.O. lectured Officers at S.B.Bn. Ration supplied 4 Offs + 210 O.R. for work on L2. Coys Commrs. inspected work	G.R.
	25th		450 men on footpaths. 250 Cape Cabin Siding. 200 L.2. Players in NF in the Association football Competition agst E.E. Carpenter L/Cpl. H.G. STEELE + 245 F.N. TURNER. Injuries Rifles from ENGLAND.	G.R.
	26th		2 Coys (A+B) Rested. 200 men (C+D) L2. Working party.	G.R.
	27th		Coy parade C on Rathing. Players selected in the Association football Competition won 1-0. Relieves B.52.: in "L" lines - see special Order for details.	G.R.
Hqrs + Defences MACHINE GUN FARM	28th		All Coys working on improvements of defences.	yds.
	29th			
	30th		All Coys. working on the defences. Adjutant left to proceed on special leave, + his duties taken over by 2/Lt. J.L. DAVIS.	yds.
	31st		All Coys. working on defences.	yds.

C. Manning Lt. Col.
Commanding 10th N.F.

Army Form C. 2118.

WAR DIARY
or
INTELLIGENCE SUMMARY.

(Erase heading not required.)

10 NF
Apl 20
1917

Place	Date April	Hour	Summary of Events and Information	Remarks and references to Appendices
2nd Lines ELVERDINGHE	1st		Major C. J. Allen. M.C. proceeds to ENGLAND to attend C.O's Course at ALDERSHOT. Major H. Clifford D.S.O. reported arrival, arms taken on the strength. He took over duties of 2nd in Command to the Battn.	20 G.B.
Defences H.Q. M.G. Farm			Companies devoted time to work on "L" defences.	G.B.
	2nd		C of E Church Parade for H.Q. "A" & "B" Companies at Battn H.Q. Work on "L" Defences. Considerable fall of snow during the day.	
	3rd		Nothing of importance happened and the usual work was done on defences.	G.B.
	4th		Relieved by 15th Welsh Regiment. Marched to "D" Camp.	App "A" G.B.
"D" Camp A.S.D.	5th		Bns in the morning. Moved to BOLLEZEELE. Vie Carcc. Entrained at BRANDHOEK 1pm and detrained ESQUELBECQ. Marched from ESQUELBECQ to BOLLEZEELE.	App "B" G.B.
BOLLEZEELE			2/Lt G.L. SMITH from ENGLAND reported for duty, was taken on the strength and posted to "C" Company.	
"	6th		Good Friday. Church Parade for Battalion was held in BOLLEZEELE. Sy 9pm.	G.B.
"	7th =		Company training on training area.	G.B.

Army Form C. 2118.

WAR DIARY
or
INTELLIGENCE SUMMARY.
(Erase heading not required.)

Instructions regarding War Diaries and Intelligence Summaries are contained in F.S. Regs., Part II. and the Staff Manual respectively. Title pages will be prepared in manuscript.

Place	Date	Hour	Summary of Events and Information	Remarks and references to Appendices
BOLLEZEELE	8.		Easter Sunday. Bn Church parade 9.15am. Inspection of billets by C.O. 12 noon to 1pm. Afternoon devoted to Recreational Training - final of 68th Rxx Association Football Competition was played V12 Bn. won 2-1.	G.R.
"	9th.		Morning Bn devoted to Bn training. Brigade Training Area. Afternoon 68th Rxx Cross Country Run. won by 10th N.F. Lt.Col. Lord R. hamer Crig R.O. proceeded to PARIS on Special leave. Major to Clifford D.S.O. took over Command of the Bahalion.	G.R.
"	10th.		Morning- Coy training on training Area under h.O.- Officii lactical exercises. Afternoon- inspection of gas helmets and drill.	G.R.
"	11th.		Bahalion carried on practice shoot on training Area.	Apps. C. G.R.
"	12th.		Bahalion Route- Employment of advance Rear and flank Grand. Lt.Col. haskins proceed on 1 month Special leave R.S.h. CARLISLE took over duties of R.S.h. Bn entrained ESQUELBECQ at 8am-entrained ESQUELBECQ detrained	G.R.
"	13th.		Moved by road to ESQUELBECQ POPERINGHE at 12 noon. marched to St Lawrence Camp. arrived in Camp. 1pm. Capt. G. L. Rands rejoined Bn from leave & returned into	Apps. G.R. G.R.
St Laurence Camp. G.11.C.			the afternoon.	

WAR DIARY
or
INTELLIGENCE SUMMARY.
(Erase heading not required.)

Army Form C. 2118.

Place	Date	Hour	Summary of Events and Information	Remarks and references to Appendices
St Lawrence Camp (G.4.d)	14th.		Morning = platoon training. Inspection of kit and anti-gas appliances. Afternoon. Anti-Lt Col. had Rhames C in C DSO. rejoined Battalion from leave and re-assumed command. 2/Lt Rhales = Major Clifford to duties of 2nd in Command.	G.B.
HOOGE SECTOR Left Batn. (Left Sub-Sector)	15.		Morning - One hour act = home to lunch. Relieved Bt. Batn R Sussex Regmnt. Quiet relief. The MACKINS. F. "C" Coy to Hospital kit Shell-shock. Lieut H.S. Ryse P.O. rejoined from leave. Took over duties of T.O.	App. E. G.B.
"	16.		From 2/Lt. A.D. Ferguson = Relief Complete 2.30 am. Generally quiet day. Weather fair. Some snow showers herenot too clearn & men have working throughout the day in clearing up.	G.B.
"	17.		Lochs has in an exceptionally peaceful mood and hardly considered that he had gone back = Rose dispositions were changed and 2 Battalions (B.D.r. & N.F.) took the line; he moves out to the r.gw taking over WARRINGTON locality from 11 N.F. move complete at 6.45 p.m.	App. F. G.B.

Disposition of the Battns: Right C. Bn. A.D.S.S./Forms/C.2118. A Suppt. D. Reserve. B. Centre F. DYKE Right... Left T. REID. Yetterx to Jn Battalions

WAR DIARY
or
INTELLIGENCE SUMMARY

Army Form C. 2118.

Place	Date	Hour	Summary of Events and Information	Remarks and references to Appendices
LEFT R at HOOGE SECTOR	18.		Again we had a quiet day. the weather has from 10.R. has been relieved by G.S. in the R. at RATION DUMP. No slight alteration has made in Coy dispositions.	G.B. App G.
"	19.		Enemy artillery has more active to-day. Lincoln St. has knocked hit Bd. 2 points OXFORD St. at 36 Crap "B". Only two direct hits could be detected firing. By this is the casualty have a large below to look after. hostile machine gun has been somewhat above normal fire has for his points. It has the MENIN RD has reached here. "Boche" has been hit his tramway running to night much more has made between 6.45 p.m. and 8 p.m.	G.B.
"	20.		A few batteries however have been relieving a considerable amount of requisition has been carried on to-day, and considering the amount of shells he sent over, his retaliation	G.B.

WAR DIARY
or
INTELLIGENCE SUMMARY.
(Erase heading not required.)

Army Form C. 2118.

Place	Date	Hour	Summary of Events and Information	Remarks and references to Appendices
LEFT Berlin HOOGE SECTOR.	20.		Remarkably Weak: During the day he gave attention to our line at BIRR + Road. and GORDON St. in rear of BRITN St. 4 heavy howitzer shells burst in rear of WARRINGTON Rd. At 5 p.m. Our howitzers retaliated when he to means of silencing the enemy. It was known by officers in the line that an "O.P." was obtained on to T.M. emplacement. At 9 p.m. an hile Coy relief was commenced. Relief complete 2.30 a.m. 21.4.17. The Batt. to have disposed as follows. "D" right. "B" left. A. Support. in Reno 2. Locality "C" Reserve B Mn Hd. remains at HALFWAY. Hg. 2/Lt. L.A. Gibson arrived back from L.G. Instructors Course ETOUQUES. Bde School opened to-day. We detailed 246 W SWINDELL YS OR for General Course - 2/Lt. A.G. BROWN YS. O.R. for L.G. Course - Course 1s. 110 days.	Gu — App. H.

WAR DIARY
or
INTELLIGENCE SUMMARY

Army Form C. 2118.

Place	Date	Hour	Summary of Events and Information	Remarks and references to Appendices
LEFT BATTn HOOGE SEC.	21.	9 am	Chinese Wood has shelled between Halfway Ho. and GORDON Ho. Sound bearing from point I.17.c.25.55. Bg. 177° Kne. Between 9 pm and 10 pm. 25 shells were fired at LEINSTER Sq and GROUND in vicinity, a bearing B gun flash was taken from I.27.6.8½.1½. and found to be 81° (Kne). Line from flash sent to report heads. 1½ seconds. There was some movement seen in enemy front line trenches to day. Sin Weath.	C.B.
	22.		There has been some activity on the front of our aeroplane during the morning, and the enemy expended about 1000 shells of various calibres firing up to 4.2" howitzers any effect = Gordon Ho Dump on the ZILLEBEKE Road received attention at intervals during the day, but did no damage + machine gun here as usual away from slant to Ornanto = Ho. B. Keltern reported on Stasho knollen corner to day –	C.B.

WAR DIARY or INTELLIGENCE SUMMARY

Army Form C. 2118.

Place	Date	Hour	Summary of Events and Information	Remarks and references to Appendices
LEFT Bn HQ HOOGE SECTOR	22.		Two patrols. One under Capt Allan the other under 2Lt. R.A. Bus were out during the night. Copy of Capt Allan's report attached. Quiet night.	App. I. G.S.
"	23.		Artillery activity throughout the day in HILL 60. Sector. Relieved by 11 N.F. at night. Withdrew to "C" position	G.S. App. J.
SUPPORT Battn HQ HILL 60 Sector	24.	1.30 am 3.0 pm 10 pm 11.30 am	Relief Complete. Quiet night. Artillery active in HILL 60 Sector. 5 Recconnoitred HILL 60 Sector. Working parties supplied to R.E. Rge now retiring returned at night. Rge on left carried out a hurricane bombardment of Sector before him some retaliation on our line. Rge on move complete.	G.S. App. K.
"	25.		Artillery activity in HILL 60 Sector. 5.45 pm ZILLEBEKE village two shops 3 officers reconnoitred HILL 60 Sector. Working parties supplied to R.E.	G.S.
"	26.	4 officers reconnoitred HILL 60 Sector = Toilers here shelled with 5.9s between 5.30 pm and 6 pm. Two direct hits obtained but no damage done. Officers all quiet = Working parties supplied to R.E. and Tunnels (Australian). Detachment "B" 10 Company moved from BARRACKS to the ESPLANADE. Two	G.S.

Army Form C. 2118.

WAR DIARY
or
INTELLIGENCE SUMMARY.
(Erase heading not required.)

Instructions regarding War Diaries and Intelligence Summaries are contained in F.S. Regs., Part II. and the Staff Manual respectively. Title pages will be prepared in manuscript.

Place	Date	Hour	Summary of Events and Information	Remarks and references to Appendices
SUPPORTS BAWN HOOGE Sector.	27.	6.30am	Rain. Mt. TUILLERS has again shelled with 5.9s = no damage done = 3 Officers reconnoitred Hill 60 Sector = Day was quiet =	
			"C" Coy relieved "D" Coy in WELLINGTON CRESCENT - relief commencing	App. L
		8.45pm	from the ESPLANADE. Relief Complete =	
			Rain. Supplied bathing parties to R.E. and R.E. Signal Service for running Cables.	
" —	28.		Rain. Mt. has shelled at intervals during the day = Officers reconnoitred Hill 60 Sector = Warning order for relief by 69th Bde. or 2 & J/4 received =	Cab.
" —	29.	8am	Rain. Mt. shelled with 4.2. = no damage done = Preliminary orders received in J relief by 58th Bde 19th Division received. P. Town Operation Order No. hqrs. 2. 20/15. received at 11-45 pm = Battalion moving to STEENVOORDE.	Cab.
" —	30.	2.30am	Rain Operation wired to Companies = Advance parties from Other Bdes arrived at 11.20am =	App. M.
			during the morning = G.O.C. Division visited Barnes =	Cbs.
		5pm	Rain Mt. shelled with 4.2s.	

R Hanner Lieut Colonel
Commdg 10th Northd. Fus.

#353 Wt. W2544/1454 700,000 5/15 D.D.&L. A.D.S.S./Forms/C.2118.

S E C R E T   C O P Y   N O. 5

10th BATTALION NORTHUMBERLAND FUSILIERS
OPERATION ORDER No. 110.

Reference BELGIUM. Sheet 28. N. W.

1. The Battalion will be relieved by the 15th Battalion Welsh Regiment, in "L" Defences about 1-0 p.m. to-day.

2. No Garrison will evacuate their post till relieved

3. Guides from L. 2., L. 4., L. 8. (1 from "A" Company and 1 from "B" Company) and "L" 10. (REIGERSBURGH) will be at VLAMERTINGHE Cross Roads at 12-30 p.m. No guides will be sent from ELVERDINGHE.

4. On relief the Garrison of each post will move to "D" Camp independently.

5. Movement EAST of VLAMERTINGHE will be by parties not larger than four men at 50 yards interval.

6. Blankets, stores etc, will be stacked at Ration Dumps by 12-30 p.m. Those at L. 10. will be stacked inside the gates of the Chateau. Small loading parties will be left in charge.

7. Lewis Guns and ammunition will be stacked by 12-30 p.m. as follows, to be collected by limbers. 1 man from each Company to be left with them :-

   "A" Company. "B" Company and REIGERSBURGH at Machine Guns Farm Dump.
   "C" Company (Less 1 Platoon) and "D" Company at ELVERDINGHE Dump.

8. Blankets, Lewis Guns etc, will not be collected till after dark.

9. Transport arrangements have been made.

10. The same huts etc, will be taken over at "D" Camp as before, and no advance party will be sent.

11. Relief of each posts will be reported to this office either by wire or runner.

12. ACKNOWLEDGE.

                                              Langley Davis
                                      ....2nd Lt.
                                   A/Adjutant. 10th Battalion Northumberland Fusiliers.

Copy No' 1. "A" Company.
   "   " 2. "B" Company.
   "   " 3. "C" Company.
   "   " 4. "D" Company.
   "   " 5. C. O.
   "   " 6. 2nd in Command.
   "   " 7. O. C. L. 10.
   "   " 8. Office.
   "   " 9. War Diary.

4th April 1917.

App "B"

SECRET   COPY No. 9

10th BATTALION NORTHUMBERLAND FUSILIERS.
OPERATION ORDER No. 11.

Reference Sheet 28 and 27. 1/40,000.

1. The Battalion will be relieved by 14th Battalion Welsh Regiment, to-morrow.

2. 2nd Lt. P. L. DELANEY will report to the Brigade Major at G. C. d. 5. 1. at 11-30 a.m. He will report to Orderly Room for entraining state before proceeding.

3. Kit, stores, blankets etc, will be stacked outside Company Headquarters by 8-0 a.m. and loading parties left.

4. Battalion will parade on road in front of Officers' Huts ready to move off at 12-0 noon.
Order. - Headquarters, "A", "B", "C", "D".
Band will parade with the Battalion.

5. Lewis Gun Handcarts (empty) will be sent to Transport Lines and at 7-30 a.m. and march with Transport Column at 8-0 a.m. Eight men for each cart will be detailed from the Companies to whom the carts belong. Bad marchers should not be chosen. Sergeant Steele of "C" Company will be in charge of them.

6. Breakfast will be at 7-0 a.m. and dinners at 10-30 a.m.

7. Cookers will return to Transport Lines to-night. Companies will take off the dixies required for cooking breakfasts and dinners, and these will be carried to the place of entraining.

8. Transport and Lewis Gun Carts will march under Brigade Transport Officer from Transport Lines at 8-0 a.m.

9. Officers chargers to meet the train at ESQUELBECQ.

10. "Billet clean certificates" will be obtained by Companies from incoming Unit.

11. ACKNOWLEDGE.

                                                                    Langley Davis
                                                                   ....2nd Lt.
                              A/Adjutant. 10th Battalion Northumberland Fusiliers.

Copy. No' 1. "A" Company.
    "   " 2. "B" Company.
    "   " 3. "C" Company.
    "   " 4. "D" Company.
    "   " 5. C. O.
    "   " 6. 2nd in Command.
    "   " 7. T. O.
    "   " 8. Q. M.
    "   " 9. Office.
    "   " 10. War Diary.

4th April. 1917.

App. B.C

SECRET   COPY NO.........

10th BATTALION NORTHUMBERLAND FUSILIERS
OPERATION ORDER.

Reference Map. 27 N. W.

The 68th Brigade will attack on the 11th inst.

__1st Objective.__   Enemy line running from G. 3. D. 6. 3. through G.3.D.6.4.
to G. 4. C. 3. 9.

__2nd Objective.__   Line through G. 3. B. 0. 0. to G. 4. A. 3. 3.

10th Battalion Northumberland Fusiliers are allotted frontage from a line
running NORTH and SOUTH through G. 4. A. 4. 0. to MERCKEGHEM-PELDERHOUCK
Road.

1. The Battalion will attack on a two Company front, "A" and "B" Companies
    in the front line, "C" and "D" Companies in the second line. Each
    Company will be in two waves of two lines each.

    Distance between waves.   -   70 yards.
    "   "   lines.   -   10 yards.

2. Moppers-up, found by the 12th Battalion Durham Light Infantry, will follow
    the second wave.

3. "A" and "B" Companies after assaulting 1st Objective, will proceed to
    take 2nd Objective. Moppers-up and "C" and "D" Companies will halt at
    1st Objective.

4. The pace and line will be entirely regulated by the barrage. Men will
    keep 50 yards behind the barrage.

5. At Zero, barrage will creep by periodical lifts to 100 yards beyond 1st
    Objective, where it will halt for three minutes, and then creep to 100
    yards beyond 2nd Objective.
    Rate of progress - About 20 yards per minute.

6. Alternate men in second wave of each Company will carry tools.

7. On arrival at Objectives, Companies will arrange to block communication
    trenches towards enemy's next position. They must also get into touch
    with the troops on their flanks.

8. Bombing Officer will arrange for each man to carry two bombs. These will
    be collected for use by bombers as soon as the objectives have been
    gained.

9. Patrols must ascertain as soon as possible the new position and
    dispositions of the enemy.

10. Bombing Officer will establish a Bomb Dump at Farm at G. 10. A. 3. 7.
    S. A. A. Reserve will be at this point also.

11. Companies will detail 1 Officer and 4 N. C. O's to reconnoitre the assault
    trenches previously, in order to fix a mutual boundary and guiding
    points.

12. Zero time will be notified later.

                             ....Major.
                             Commanding 10th Battalion Northumberland Fusiliers.

10th April. 1917.

SECRET   App IV.   COPY NO. 7

10th BATTALION NORTHUMBERLAND FUSILIERS.
CONTINUATION OF OPERATION ORDER NO. 112.

1. The following additions are made to the Operation Order of to-night.

2. A rear party, composed of 2nd Lt. T. A. ANDERSON and 1 N. C. O. from each Company, will be left behind to hand over billets. They will report to Brigade Headquarters for orders after doing so.

3. The Battalion will parade in the Square in close column of Companies at 7-30 a.m.

4. 2nd Lt. J. O. WHYTE will report to the Staff Captain at ESQUELBECQ STATION at 9-15 a.m.

5. The Transport will march with the Battalion as far as ESQUELBECQ STATION, and thence by road to lines near BRANDHOEK, which will be notified later.

6. The Battalion will entrain at ESQUELBECQ and detrain at POPERINGHE.

7. 2nd Lt. T. A. ANDERSON will attend to any claims which may be made, by arrangements he will make with the Brigade Interpreter.

                                       .... 2nd Lt.
                         A/Adjutant. 10th Battalion Northumberland Fusiliers.

```
Copy No. 1   "A" Company.
  "    "  2   "B"    "
  "    "  3   "C"    "
  "    "  4   "D"    "
  "    "  5   T. O.
  "    "  6   Q. M.
  "    "  7   R. S. M.
  "    "  8   Office.
```

12th April. 1917.

SECRET   COPY NO'........

10th BATTALION NORTHUMBERLAND FUSILIERS
OPERATION ORDER NO' 113.

1. The Battalion will relieve 13th Battalion Royal Sussex Regiment in Left sub-Sector of HOOGE Sector to-morrow night, 15th April.

2. **Dispositions**, will be as follows :-
   - Right Front Company. "C" (From Gap "A" to Gap "B")
     - 2 Platoons in BOND STREET.
     - 2 Platoons in ROSSLYN STREET.
   - Left Front Company. "A" (From Gap "B" exclusive to BIRR X Road.)
     - 3 Platoons in Front Line.
     - 1 Platoon in CULVERT.
   - Support Company. "D" 3 Platoons in LEINSTER STREET.
     - 1 Platoon in ROSSLYN STREET.
   - Reserve Company. "B" 2 Platoons in HALFWAY HOUSE.
     - 1 Platoon in RAILWAY CUTTING.

   Battalion Headquarters.   -   HALFWAY HOUSE.
   Regimental Aid Post.   -   HALFWAY HOUSE.

3. The Battalion will parade at 7-30 p.m. and will entrain at BRANDHOEK 8-15 p.m. Train departs 8-45 p.m.
   Order of march :- H. Q. "C", "A", "D", "B" Company.
   Guides will be at MENIN GATE at 9-30 p.m.
   Route via MENIN ROAD.

4. Movement after detrainment will be by platoons at 100 yards distance. All movement EAST of VLAMERTINGHE by daylight in parties not larger than 4 men at 50 yards distance.

5. O. C. "B" Company will detail an Officer to precede the Battalion by 15 minutes to acquaint himself with exact point of entrainment. He will report to the Staff Captain at BRANDHOEK STATION immediately on arrival there.

6. Lewis Gunners will accompany their respective Companies.

7. All baggage, blankets etc, for conveyance to the line and Q. M. Stores, will be stacked outside the Guard Room and Medical Inspection Room respectively, by 5-30 p.m. Loading parties will be detailed by Officers Commanding Company.

8. The following will be taken over from the outgoing Unit :-
   Trench and R. E. Stores, Defence Schemes, Log-Books, Maps, air photo's and statement of work in progress and proposed.
   Receipts for stores will be forwarded to Battalion Headquarters by 10-0 a.m on 16th inst.

9. Advance party will proceed in accordance with warning order from BRANDHOEK at 9-0 p.m. to-day.

10. No lorries or baggage wagons will be available for the transport of baggage to-morrow.

11. Completion of reliefs will be reported to Battalion Headquarters by code.

12. ACKNOWLEDGE.

                                                       George Armd
                                                       Captain and Adjutant.
14th April. 1917.   10th Battalion Northumberland Fusiliers.

Issued at 7-0 p.m.

SECRET.

FILE Wulton

Operation Order No 114

1. Reference Warning Order issued to you under this office No O.R. 2/p dated 16th inst.

2. The relief will commence from the left flank of the line at 8.30 pm today and positions as laid down in para 2 will be taken up.

3. "C" Company will not move until relieved by "A" Coy.

4. O.C. "C" Coy will establish a Bombing post of 1 N.C.O. and men at junction of I.20.9 and I.B.1. This point will be the meeting place for the patrols from the 2 front Companies. The party will be posted by an officer and will take tools to improve the trench.

5. Ration dumps will be as follows.
    "A" Coy 3 platoons HELLFIRE Cr   1 platoon GORDON Ho
    "B" "   GORDON Ho Dump
    "D" "   GORDON Ho Dump   "C" Coy ZILLEBEKE Dump

"B" "C" & "D" Companies will supply their own carrying parties. "D" Coy will in addition carry for "A" Company.

Trench Stores and Log Books will remain as at present & Lewis Guns will be allotted as follows.
"A" Coy 6 guns (2 guns as at present & 2 guns "B" Coy & 2 in BOND?)
New Bond & Wieltje front to "B" Coy   2 in Railway Ho
"C" 4 guns WARRINGTON Locality D'pts as present
Guns will be readjusted accordingly.
Completion of relief will be reported. George Bond

Secret
Copy

Reference Battalion Operation Order 113 dated 19th
Ipswic para 7. The dispositions of Lewis Guns after
relief will be as follows:—

Location	Guns	Company
The CULVERT	2 Guns	"B" Company
Culvert Locality, front line	1 "	"B" "
	1 "	"C" "
Bond Street Locality, 2 line	2 Guns	"A" Company
" " Rear of Coy "B"	1 "	"C" "
LEINSTER Street	1 "	"A" "
ROSSLYN Street	1 "	"A" "
Warrington Av. Locality front line	4 "	"D" "
HALFWAY St	1 "	"C" "
Railway Cutting	1 "	"C" "

RELIEF OF GUNS

The two Guns "B" Company in HALFWAY St and
Railway Cutting will move at 8 pm but no other
Gun will move until relieved. Moves will be as
per table as under:—

MOVE FROM	MOVE TO and RELIEVE
2 Guns "B" Coy HALFWAY St & Rly Cg	2 Guns "A" Coy CULVERT
2 " "A" " CULVERT	2 " "D" Coy LEINSTER St and ROSSLYN St
" "D" Coy LEINSTER & ROSSLYN S.	2 Guns "C" Coy WARRINGTON Av
" "C" " WARRINGTON AV	1 Gun "B" Coy BOND St
	1 " "A" " F.L. CULVERT Loc
" "B" " BOND St	1 " "A" " " "
" "A" " F.L. CULVERT Loc	2 " "D" " " BOND St Loc
" "D" " BOND St Loc	2 " "C" " WARRINGTON Loc
" "D" " F.L. WARRINGTON	2 " "B" " HALFWAY St & Rly Cg

SECRET.

10th Battalion. Nor'd. Fusiliers

WARNING ORDER.

1. The following alterations in present dispositions will be made tomorrow night April 17th.

2. The Battalion will be disposed as follows:-

   CULVERT LOCALITY   3 platoons "A" Coy.
   BOND ST LOCALITY   1   "   "   "A"   "

   WARRINGTON LOCALITY

      Front line   3   "   "   "C"   "
      Lovers Walk   1   "   "   "C"   "

   LEINSTER STREET   3   "   "   "D"   "
   ROSSLYN ST at
   Junction with Bond St.)   1   "   "   "D"   "

   HALFWAY HOUSE   - Battalion H.Q.
   and RAILWAY CUTTING   "B" Coy - as at present.

3. Further details will be issued tomorrow, but O.C. Coys. should arrange for reconnaissance of new positions to be made by a proportion of their Officers & N.C.O's tomorrow morning.

4. Arrangements are to be made for Officers to be in close touch with their Platoons. The Coy Commanders will remain with the major part of their Coys; 2nd's in Command with the minor parts.

5. Acknowledge.

George Lund
Capt - Adjt

15-4-17.

10th BATTALION NORTHUMBERLAND FUSILIERS.

Secret.
/: App G.

The following alterations in
dispositions will be carried out
tonight. Arrangements will be
made between the Company Commanders
concerned.

1 platoon "D" Coy from LEINSTER St
will take over BOND St Locality
from 1 platoon "A" Coy.

The platoon "A" Coy on relief
will move from Bond St Locality
to LEINSTER St. taking up a
position at North end of LEINSTER St
in Support to CULVERT Locality Garrison.
Position taken up will be East of
LEINSTER FARM.

The Q.M. will arrange for the
whole of "A" Coy's rations to be dumped
at HELLFIRE CORNER.

Reliefs will be reported to Batn. HQ.
ACKNOWLEDGE.
George Bandt Capt

There will be no movements until 8.45pm

ORDERLY ROOM
No. 71
18 APR 1917
1/R8

SECRET.
Copy Appendix IV.

Copy No.

Battalion Operation Order No. 118.

1. "B" and "D" Companies will relieve "A" and "C" Companies respectively on the night of 20th April.

2. The reliefs will be carried out as follows:-
"B" Company will move from RAILWAY No to CULVERT LOCALITY at 9 p.m.
"A" Company on relief will withdraw to Support positions and move to BOND St locality.
"D" Company on relief will move to WARRINGTON LOCALITY
"C" Company on relief will withdraw to RESERVE position

3. Trench-Stores, log-books, maps and defence Schemes will be handed over.

4. There will be as little movement as possible before dark.

5. Further details of relief will be arranged between Company Commanders

6. A proportion of officers and NCOs will reconnoitre positions tomorrow morning

7. Distribution of Lewis Guns will be notified later.

8. Ration-parties will be supplied as follows:
"C", "A", and "D" Companies will arrange their own parties. "A" Company will in addition carry for "B" Coy.

9. Disposition reports will be rendered to Battn HQ by 9 a.m. on 21st inst.

10. Completion of reliefs will be reported

11. ACKNOWLEDGE.

George Baird.
CAPT & ADJUTANT

Copies to OC. C. Companies. T.O. Q.M.
C.O. Indus C. Aft. L.G.O.
Office War Diary Signal

HOPE

To. 64th Inf. Brigade Hqrs.

Report on Patrol

A patrol of 1 officer + 2 men left the CULVERT at dusk with the object of lying in wait for any small party of the enemy that might emerge from supposed sally-port at I.18.B.d.44 in order to obtain identification.

They reached the enemy wire unobserved. A sentry could be seen to the left of the sally port & a machine gun was fired once from this point I.18.B.15.45. Very lights were fired from this point & also from I.18.B.14.35.

The two men were left under the enemy wire while the officer reconnoitred to the right to find a gap in the wire. He was seen & heard & the enemy threw two bombs from right sentry post I.18.B.14.35. He returned & reconnoitred to the left. The wire was concertina barbed & not thick but there was no gap. On his return the men reported that one or two of the enemy had come out through the sally-port into what appeared to be a short sap or advanced trench. They could be heard talking & walking about. They fired a Very light which appeared to come from the ground level. Our patrol then threw three bombs & withdrew 50 yds. & the enemy apparently took cover. Soon after an angry voice was heard, presumably an officer ordering them out again. A party of 6 or 8 men ran out to the end of the sap, which appeared to be just inside the wire. The enemy showed no inclination to come through their wire & the patrol returned to the CULVERT about 1.15 a.m. About half-an-hour later 20 to 30 bombs were thrown near the sally port & single bombs were thrown at intervals for some time after.

There was a M.G. firing from the left of road along enemy wire.

J Langley Davis Lt
for O.C. 10th N.F.

23.4.17.

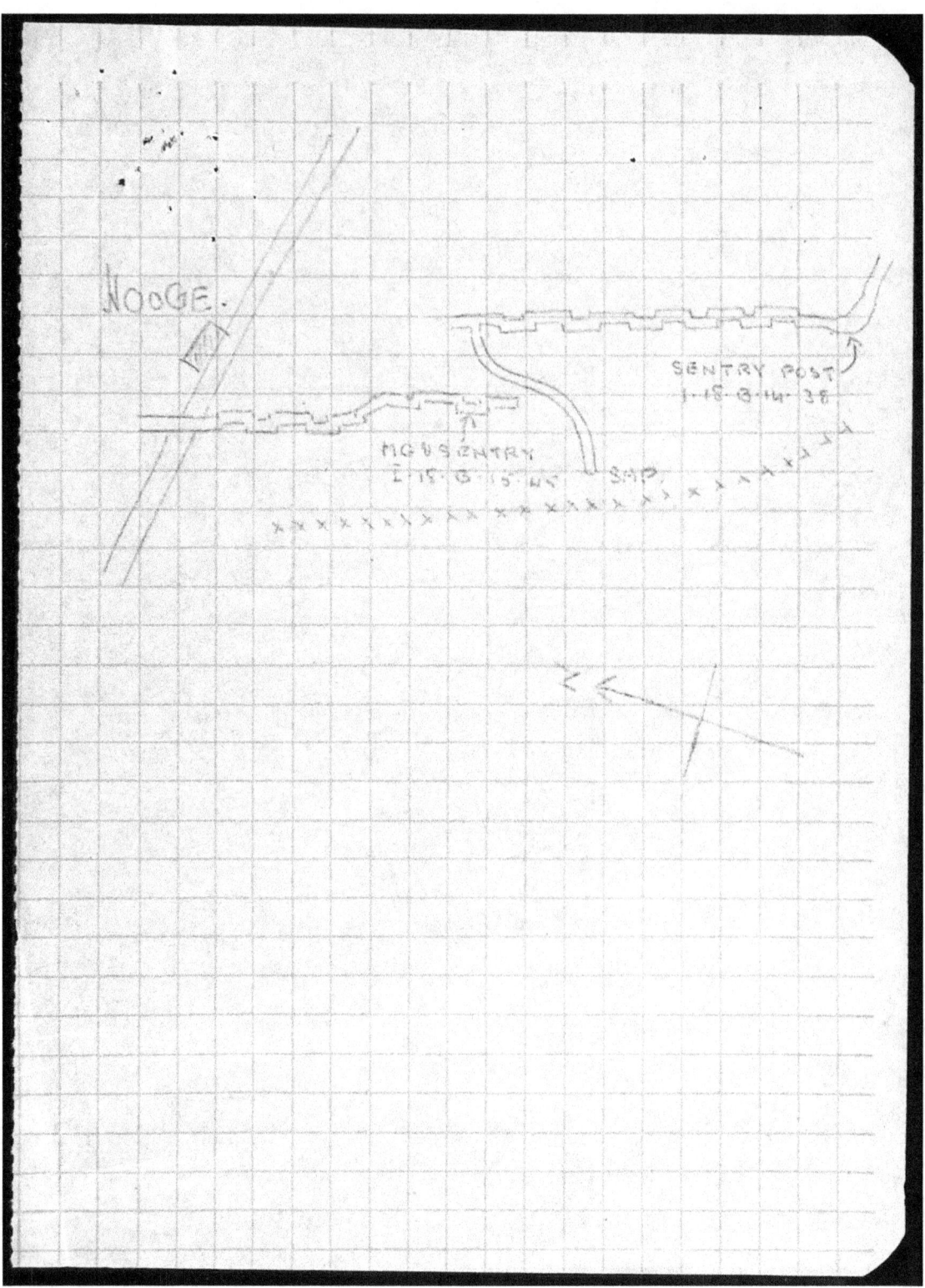

SECRET   Copy No.

10th Batn. Northd: Fusiliers:
Operation Order No 117

1. The Battalion will be relieved by 11th Batn Northd:
Fusiliers in the Left Subsector Hooge Sector tomorrow
22nd April and on relief will withdraw to the
Support positions Hooge Sector.

2. The Battalion will be disposed as follows:—

    Battalion Headqrs. "The Tuileries"

   "A" Coy.   Ritz Street   taking over from "A" Coy 11.N.F
   "B" "   (less 1 pln) WELLINGTON CRES.   "   "   "   "B" "   "
   "C" "   INF: BARRACKS YPRES   "   "   "   "D" "   "
   "D" "   (2 platoons) WELLINGTON CRES. "   "   "   "C" "   "
            (2 platoons) MAPLE Street.

3. All trench baggage will be carried to the
new positions under Company arrangements,
except that "C" Company's will be conveyed on
empty ration limbers.

4. Ration Dump for Batn HQ and "A", "B" and "D" Companies
will be the ZILLEBEKE Dump.

5. No guides will be required by the incoming unit.

6. Advance parties of 1 off per Coy, 1 N.C.O. per platoon
and 2 N.C.O.s per Batn HQ will proceed to
take over tomorrow morning. All stores, work log
books etc. will be taken over, also detail of working parties

7. Completion of reliefs will be reported.

22 APR 1917

                                        Captn. & Adjt.
                                10TH (S) BATTN. NORTHD. FUSILIERS.

SECRET.   COPY NO. 12.

10th BATTALION NORTHUMBERLAND FUSILIERS

OPERATION ORDER NO. 118.

Ref. Map. ZILLEBEKE. 1: 10,000.

1. The following moves will take place in the Support positions to-night 24th/25th April.

    (a) 2 Platoons "D" Company in MAPLE STREET will be relieved by 2 Platoons 11th N. F. and will move to WELLINGTON CRESCENT in relief of "B" Company (less 1 Platoon.)

    (b) "B" Company (less 1 Platoon) on relief will withdraw to INFANTRY BARRACKS, YPRES.

2. On completion of moves the Battalion will be disposed as follows :-

    "D" Company.   -   WELLINGTON CRESCENT.

    "A" Company.   -   RITZ STREET.

    "B" Company.   -   (less 1 Platoon)   , INFANTRY BARRACKS.

    "C" Company.   -   INFANTRY BARRACKS.

    BATTALION HEADQUARTERS.   -   TUILLERIES.

    R. A. P.   -   ZILLEBEKE.

3. No position will be vacated until occupied by Units in accordance with para 1 (a).

4. Officers valises and blankets for "B" Company, will be sent to the BARRACKS to-night.

5. Particulars re re-allotment of working parties will be notified later.

6. The usual stores, maps and log-books will be handed over.

7. Sick of "B" and "C" Companies will attend R. A. P. at INFANTRY BARRACKS.

8. Advanced parties will proceed to take over new positions this afternoon.

9. Completion of moves will be reported.

10. ACKNOWLEDGE.

George Lund
Captain and Adjutant.
10th Battalion Northumberland Fusiliers.

Copy No. 1. "A" Company.   Copy No. 5. T. O.   Copy No. 9.
  "   " 2. "B"   "   "   " 6. Q. M.   "   " 10.
  "   " 3. "C"   "   "   " 7. L. G. O.   "   " 11.
  "   " 4. "D"   "   "   " 8. Signals.   "   " 12.

                   Copy No. 13. Office.

24th April. 1917.

SECRET   COPY N0.

10th BATTALION NORTHUMBERLAND FUSILIERS

OPERATION ORDER NO. 119.

1. "C" Company will relieve "D" Company in WELLINGTON CRESCENT to-night, details to be arranged between Company Commanders.

2. Relief will commence from the ESPLANADE at 8-45 p.m.

3. Usual trench stores and details of working parties will be taken over.

4. Formation on route by sections at 100 yards distance.

5. Completion of relief will be reported to Battalion Headquarters in Code.

6. ACKNOWLEDGE.

George Laud.
....
Captain and Adjutant.
10th Battalion Northumberland Fusiliers.

```
Copy No' 1. "A" Company. )
   "    " 2. "B"    "    ) For information.
   "    " 3  "C"    "
   "    " 4  "D"    "
   "    " 5  Transport Officer.
   "    " 6  Quartermaster.
   "    " 7. Major Clifford. D. S. O.
   "    " 8. Office.
   "    " 9. War Diary.
```

27th April. 1917.

App. 17

BATTALION OPERATION ORDERS.
No. 180.

1. .... will be relieved in our support position north .... by the 13th Battalion .... Regiment on the night of 30th April/1st May, 1917, and .... will proceed to GODEWAERSVELDE.

2. Battalion H.Q. and "B" and "D" Companies will entrain at YPRES at 3-0 a.m. on 1st May, and detrain at GODEWAERSVELDE proceeding from detraining point to STEENVOORDE by route march.

"A" and "C" Companies under Major .... CLIFFORD D.S.O. will entrain at .... at .... to-day, together with the 13th D.L.I. Major .... will be in general charge of detachment on the 13th D.L.I. Train. Platoon guides, 1 guide per platoon, under an officer will await the arrival at the detraining unit.

3. Battalion H.Q. A and C Companies will not move until relieved.

4. Platoon guides from each Company and 3 per Headquarters will report to 2nd Lieut. ...... DAVIS at YPRES siding about H. 12 Central at 8-10 p.m. to-day.

5. All Trench Maps, "Fiched", Defence Schemes, Trench Stores and other documents will be handed over and receipts in duplicate will be taken and forwarded to Battalion Headquarters as soon as possible after Relief. The attention of Company Commanders is drawn to Battalion Order No. 4 dated 28th inst.

6. The 1st Line Transport will march at 3-5 p.m. to-day under Brigade Transport Officer in accordance with instructions handed to Transport Officer yesterday. 2nd Lieut. A. C. FERGUSON will remain in charge rear party.

7. Three lorries are allotted to the Battalion. Two lorries will be at the BRASSERIE and .... DUMP, at 10-0 a.m. to-day, at which hour officers valises, blankets and majority of mess stores will be stacked and loaded into lorries.
For the purpose of moving kit and stores of H. Q. "A" and "C" Companies, 3 L.G.S. wagons and Maltese Cart will be at ZILLEBEKE Dump at 10-30 p.m. to-day. One of the three L.G.S. wagons will call at the BRASSERIE on its way out to pick up remaining mess stores of the detachment.
Lorries will proceed to the office of the TOWN MAJOR, STEENVOORDE.
Transport wagons mentioned in this para. will remain at the present lines for night of 30th April/1st May, and proceed to STEENVOORDE on morning of 1st prox. under 2nd Lieut. A. C. FERGUSON.

8. ALL S.A.A. Boxes will be collected at Battalion and Company H.Q. and handed over in bulk.

9. Airdrome parties will proceed in accordance with this office number 103/802 of yesterday.

10. Lewis Guns of all Companies will remain at GODEWAERSVELDE under guard. The Transport Officer will arrange for two limbers to be sent to detraining station at 4-0 a.m. 1st prox. for their collection and transport of same to STEENVOORDE.
The Lewis Gun handcarts will not be taken to the new area.

11. The Mess Cart and officers chargers for H. Q. "A" and "C" Companies will be at detraining station at 4-0 a.m. on 1st prox.

12. Completion of reliefs will be reported.

13. ACKNOWLEDGE.

George Lund
Captain and Adjutant.

30th April 1917.

Copies 1 - 4. O's. C. Companies.
   " 5 - 9. H. Q. Staff.
   " 10. Transport Officer.   13. Office.
   " 11. Quartermaster.   14. War Diary.
   " 12. Signals Officer.

10 N F
96 21
21
1917

WAR DIARY
or
INTELLIGENCE SUMMARY.
(Erase heading not required.)

Army Form C. 2118.

Place	Date	Hour	Summary of Events and Information	Remarks and references to Appendices
STEENVOORDE TRAINING AREA.	MAY 1st	3 am	Battalion entrained at YPRES.	G.B.
		5 am	Arrived GODEWAERSVELDE & marched to STEENVOORDE area.	
		6 am	Arrived in billets.	
			Rifle & Min. parade in the afternoon.	
	2nd		Company inspections held in the morning.	G.B.
		2.15pm	G.O.C. 2nd Div. visited Batt.	
	3rd	—	Company training - "A" Coy. rifle range	G.B.
			Drill - Attack Exercise - maintenance.	
	4th		Company training - "B" Coy rifle range -	G.B.
			Drill - Attack Exercise - Outpost Scheme - Route march -	
	5th		Battalion Exercise.	G.B.
	6th		Church parades. Cos inspections & billets in the morning.	G.B.
			Bn. Rapid & Reserve fired by F.G.C.M. 5 - 30 pm.	
	7th		American Forward Communication =	App B. 91
			Mad Battalion Exercises. Due Sparts =	

Army Form C. 2118.

WAR DIARY
or
INTELLIGENCE SUMMARY.
(Erase heading not required.)

Place	Date	Hour	Summary of Events and Information	Remarks and references to Appendices
STEENVOORDE TRAINING AREA	8.		Battalion Exercise - Battalion Resting throughout =	
	9.		Move to ST LAWRENCE CAMP = Arrived in Camp at 12.15 pm	Sa App 'C' App 'D' G.S.
	10.		Move to Right Subsection - HULL 66 Sector = Quiet evening	G.S.
RIGHT Subn HULL 66 Sect	11.	7am	Relief Complete = Quiet N.A.Js S.P.Gs observed ret. S.G. at 7pm = again at 2pm until 3pm. No ammunition - Casualties NIL = Wire here intelligent = artillery fire hurried to draw But on the whole everything has remained quiet.	G.S.
"	12.		Nothing of importance to record. 2Lt. L.A. Gibson took on a patrol at 9.45pm to examine body of an Australian lying in No Mans Land at I. 34. 6. 95. 30. No identification here found. Quiet night. 7pm British aeroplane fire, out Rear of a SqW, into the German lines on our left at K.5. in Sam B.3am D.J.1 The left Subsector here raided. Our line heavy.	G.S.
"	13.		WINDY CORNER Pol received Orders attention during this enterprise. Aeroplane activity here above normal throughout the day = "D" Coy relieved "B" Coy in the evening =	App E.

WAR DIARY or INTELLIGENCE SUMMARY

Army Form C. 2118.

Place	Date	Hour	Summary of Events and Information	Remarks and references to Appendices
RIGHT BY HILL 60 S.C.	14.		The day was quite quiet. "Y" Coy relieved "C" in TOW front Coy position. Relief complete 10.30 p.m. 2 officers' patrols went out from "y" & "D" Companies at 11.30 p.m. under 2/Lt. B. McCAN & 2/Lt. T. C. BROWNE. Patrols were opposed and the "A" Coy patrol was forced to withdraw owing to offr. M-G. & rifle fire. 2/Lt BROWNE raided wire in front of enemy's line.	App "F" GW
	15.		Was quiet. Wire reconnoitred at 2.30 p.m. no casualties. IMPACT trench. Patrol returned at 2.30 p.m. no casualties. A fairly quiet day with exception of two short periods of shelling of S.P. Q. between 10-45 a.m. and 11-15 a.m. & 8p.m. - B- & p.m. Our S.Q. caribou was employed on all about 30 shells burst in the vicinity – no damage was done. Our Rifle Grenadiers carried our registration on IMPACT trenches and Serville points in the enemy's front and C/Sgt. aim Offrs. inj.= 35. Grenadiers were fired with good results. One hour fired poots on	GW KILLED 2/Lt L.O.R. 4 G WOUNDED 30R.T.C. 2 B G
	16.		New enemy trenches on WIL GP. Quiet night with the exception of hostile M-Gun activity at Klein.To. A bombardment on our left commenced aimed about 30 minutes.	GB

WAR DIARY
or
INTELLIGENCE SUMMARY.
(Erase heading not required.)

Army Form C. 2118.

Place	Date	Hour	Summary of Events and Information	Remarks and references to Appendices
Point By Sec. 66 Sec. 16			Our line received a little attention during the bombardment =	Killed 1 O.R. Wound M.A.
			Reg. Sgt. Burrell of "A" Coy. was killed by shrapnel, and	1 O.R. W
			one man of "A" Coy. wounded.	
			Captain R.S.B. reported his return & was later on to	
			assume command of "A" Coy. from Capt. T.L. Allan.	
			Strength: The Roots were subjected to intense Bombardment at 3.20 p.m.	
	17.		Quiet morning. Lines opened fire S.P.9.	Casualties
		4.40 p.m. and 9.15 p.m. Special attention was given to	4 killed
			Sunken Road, Cruces Diagonal, & left to	16 wounded
			Our guns retaliated on each of the 3 occasions. His was more	
			considerable, as I was thought his own having which	
			here firing continuously causes he has much annoyance &	G.A.G
			consequently there & shortly here retaliation on his part.	
			1 mine was blown under hill 60 at 10.14 p.m. no apparent action	
			followed though at 10.55 p.m. a small party works towards	
			our left post in the CUTTING, but were driven off by bombers =	
			The relief by 10th West R. Regt. was performed from 17/16 to 16/9.	

… Army Form C. 2118.

WAR DIARY
or
INTELLIGENCE SUMMARY.
(Erase heading not required.)

Place	Date	Hour	Summary of Events and Information	Remarks and references to Appendices
RIGHT BANK HILL 60.	18.		The day was quiet until 6.15 p.m. when enemy opened a gas on S.P.9. Attk.	
			Caithro up to and including 21 Cpn. Several dug-outs were blown in, and through the hundred dug-outs casualties were received	G.S.
			H.Q.15 from the 15th Hs Ridents was arriving. 6yd relief has been delayed owing to the late arrival of Westminis Simo=	App "G"
VANCOUVER CAMP=	19=	2.30 a.m.	Relief has complete.	
		5 a.m.	Bataivio had arrived in Camp. Good accommodation. Capt Lincoln. M.C. rejoined Bn. draft of 92 taken on strength.	G.S.
	20.		Church parade. Route of engineer held on "B" Coys Cask but postponed fr further documentary evidence = draft of trained shoeing smiths supplied to R.E. S.Annes.	G.S.
	21.		Returns sent by F.O.C.H. at St Annes Camp= holding pady of 100 supplied to R.E. Signals. draft of 33. O.R. arrived from at WINNIPEG. Camp. draft of 70 arrived.	G.S.
	22.		"C" & "D" Companies relieved 2 Coys 13 B.L in 2 H.E.&R.E. Runs for work under C.R.E.	App "H"

A6945 Wt. W14422/M1160 350,000 12/16 D.D. & L. Forms/C./2118/14.

WAR DIARY
or
INTELLIGENCE SUMMARY.
(Erase heading not required.)

Army Form C. 2118.

Place	Date	Hour	Summary of Events and Information	Remarks and references to Appendices
VANCOUVER Camp.	23.		Working parties of 250 in April for carrying T.M. Ammunition.	Cal.
"	24		No working parties provided. Tea "A" "B" Companies all refitted. Lifa Gun Inspiration. F.S. 41 - 927. % OR. T.S. 27 % 624.	
"	25		"A" & "B" Coys. See ballot	
"	26		Working Parties provided - Nothing further to report.	
"	27		Quiet day except "C" + "D" Companies to ford VANCOUVER CAMP. Shelled whilen open and 3 men SOH. V. Shells to damage	Cal.
"	28		"C" "D" Companies returned at the Band & returned to Scottish	Trikes
"	29		LINES. Working party of 100 men provided = VANCOUVER camp. Shelled at intervals during the night. Parades during to any working parties: Adj' 47 arrived.	App I
"	30.		Lt. Col. S. log latters Baker relieved 6 Yorks R Gurs Subaltern Att d Co Sects 2	AppJ =

WAR DIARY
or
INTELLIGENCE SUMMARY.
(Erase heading not required.)

Army Form C. 2118.

Place	Date	Hour	Summary of Events and Information	Remarks and references to Appendices
R.C. Sub Sec.				
HILL 60	31.	1. A.M.	Relief Complete. Remainder quiet relief.	
		3.30 P.M.	Enemy opened fire on the RAVINE WOOD with a barry of 5.9.	
		3.45	Shelling ceased. 50 shells fired.	
		10 A.M.	Our heavies (6") bombarded enemy's support trenches from T.35.A.45.20 to T.35.a.27.00. Our signal Coy "D" evacuated	GR
			front line prob- Shelling continued throughout to hospital and afternoon.	
			Working party of 70 men provided for R.E. arrie longer.	

Manners Lt Colonel.
Comdg 1st North'd Fus.

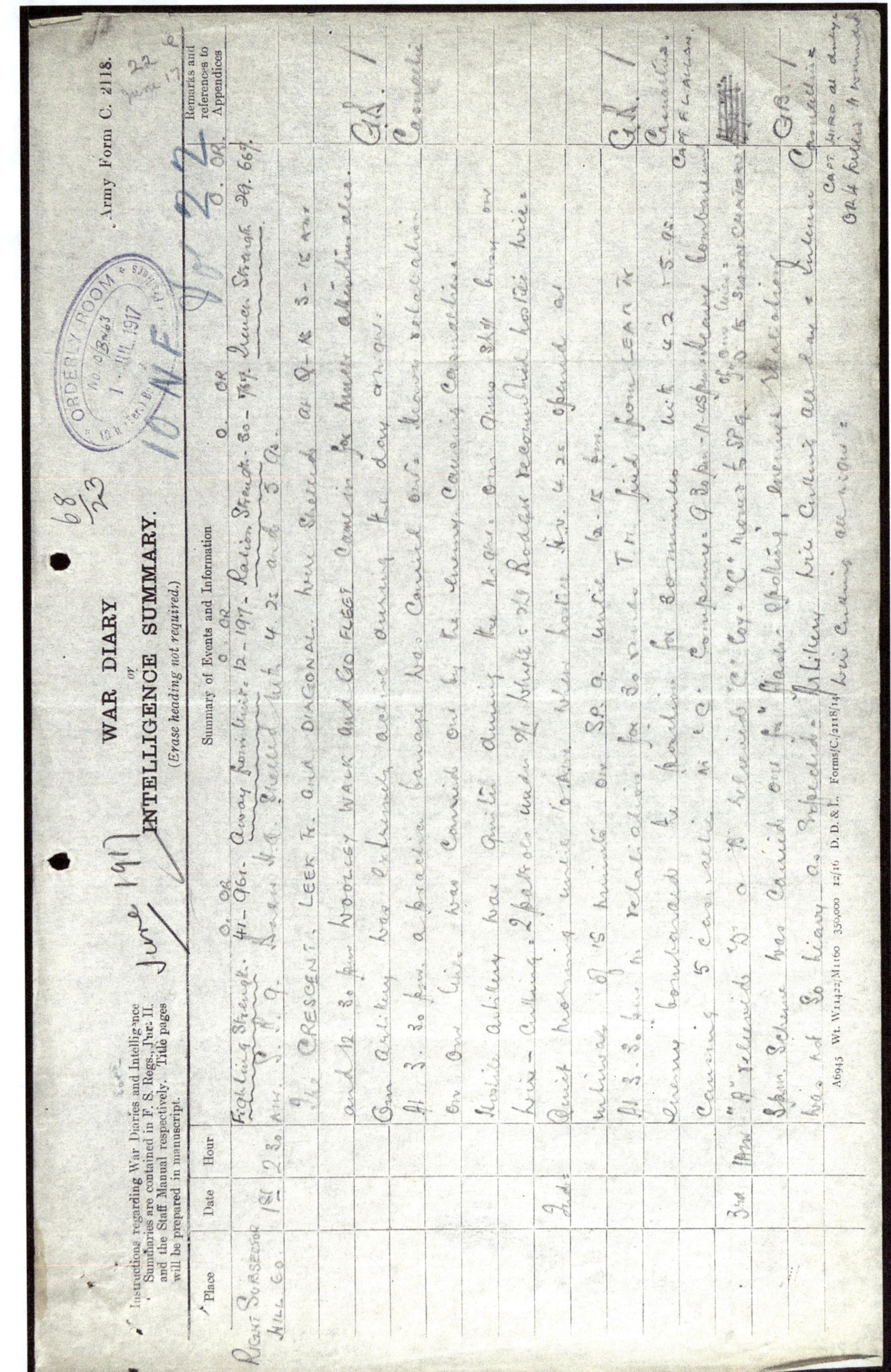

WAR DIARY or INTELLIGENCE SUMMARY

Army Form C. 2118.

Place	Date	Hour	Summary of Events and Information	Remarks and references to Appendices
Right Sector Hill 60	3rd		Quiet afternoon and evening until 9.15 broken from our support line heavy shell. One gun retaliated effectively. His	
			Gendarmerie was repeated at midnight and 2am	
			Gun F-photographic carried on by artillery a/c R.F.C. from 3pm - 3.30pm. Our patrols reconn'd Orcarge wire from 11 pm - 12.30 am.	
			No 1 patrol under 2/Lt. Ray. No 2 patrol under 2/Lt. Hotchinson	a/d
			Spent time hunting on his front line parapet in	
			large numbers. Casualties up to 12 noon 3rd June xxxxx Nebig O.R.	
			4 killed 11 wounded. Capt. Hirde severely wounded at xxxxx	
	4th		2am enemy combated our positions and again at 3 am. no damage done. On the whole morning was Quiet. Our own active cutting his	
			enemy xxxxx had put some live wire ov. opposite WINDY C	Cas xxxx
			before "stands to" in the morning.	O.R.
			Casualties to hour = 3 killed 7 wounded	3 kld 7 wnd
			Considerable Artillery activity on our right as to xxxx	
	5th		Day was Quiet. At about 9pm a convoy of Abbey G.S. wagons	
			came up the valley towards the Sunken Road on nearing S.P. of Key Ave	

Army Form C. 2118.

WAR DIARY
or
INTELLIGENCE SUMMARY.
(Erase heading not required.)

Instructions regarding War Diaries and Intelligence Summaries are contained in F.S. Regs., Part II. and the Staff Manual respectively. Title pages will be prepared in manuscript.

Place	Date	Hour	Summary of Events and Information	Remarks and references to Appendices
RIGHT Bn MU 60.	5		Spotted Enemy Guns observed S.O.S. Cannein for an intense Shelling from 9 to 9-15 pm - after this all was quiet.	
"	6		The Battalion has been relieved by 16th B. Rings. moved back to "P. Camp". 3 Cossacks in "B" Coy on the way out = Enemy was	GR
"			Shelling back area and batteries with H.V. Guns 5.9 and Gas	
"P. Camp"			Shells. Making things unpleasant & a doing no serious damage.	GR
			Occasionally one or two of Range heat up =	
			Batteries had arrived in "P. Camp" by 5.30am and during the day - preparations for the Tr. line were made.	Apps.A.
		10.15	have commenced to RAILWAY Aug - onts.	
Son				
Reserve Line	7th			
Reserve Line	8th		} Situation See Appendix B	App.B. + 8
23rd Div.	9th			GR
	10th		Bann has arrived in "P. Camp" in 4.30am.	
			Recvd. Capt. E.T. DYKE (No.1) 2Lt. DAVIS to hospital sick = Capt. DE SCOTT. Lieut. Owen duties of Plato nCr DYKE (Sick).	GR

WAR DIARY
or
INTELLIGENCE SUMMARY.
(Erase heading not required.)

Army Form C. 2118.

Place	Date	Hour	Summary of Events and Information	Remarks and references to Appendices
"P" Camp	11.		Recto. Six days Refield and Rabie inspection. Arrival WINNIPEG	
"	12.		G.O.C. 23rd Divn. addressed the Battalion at 10.45am. Capt. Lincoln to hospital with mumps. Onto the Divisional A.D. Signals Battalion moved to DICKEBUSCH to billet the Battalion.	App "a"
DICKEBUSCH				
	13.		X Corps for burying Cables. Working party of 2 Offrs & 500 O.R. provided; marched from camp at 10 a.m; returned to Camp 6.30 p.m.	
"	14.		Working party 2 Offrs 500 O.R. Supplied. Marched from camp at 9.30 a.m; returned to camp 4 p.m.	
"	15.		Wire Parties provided. Worked by day.	
"	16.		Wire Parties provided. Worked by day. Night Relieved early owing to heavy shelling.	
"	17.		"	
			Party came under hostile Artillery fire as on previous night but completed the task. Casualties 1 O.R. killed 1 O.R. wounded. Cochranue proceded on leave to ENGLAND. Major O.C. Clifford took over command of the Battalion.	
"	18.		Thunderstorm during the afternoon. Parties worked by night.	

WAR DIARY
or
INTELLIGENCE SUMMARY.
(Erase heading not required.)

Army Form C. 2118.

Place	Date	Hour	Summary of Events and Information	Remarks and references to Appendices
DICKEBUSCH	JUNE 1917 19		Moved party marched by day	AB
"	20		Camp shelled. Major W Clifford D.S.O. Coy's Adjutant & R Read killed at 10.30am and were buried at DICKEBUSCH MILITARY CEMETERY at 3p.m. 2pm Spares	
			A.2.3.B.30.60 (Sheet 28 N.W. BELGIUM Edition 4B Trench) Lieut C.E Savage badly wounded at some time & died at 6.30pm at C.C.S. LCp.R killed 6 O.R. wounded	
			Captain H.E.O. Foster took over command 2Lt J.R. Spain returned from hostile & took over duties of adjutant.	
"	21		Relieved by 2nd D.L.I. at 4pm went to THIEUSHOUK by motor lorries	
THIEUSHOUK	22		Company training	
"	23		Battalion fired on range	
"	24		Baths 9 – 12 noon Voluntary Church Parade in afternoon	
"	25		Baths 9 – 12 noon Company of Specialist training	
"	26		Company & Specialist training	
"	27		Brigade parade in H.pi. field 10.30am Major Gen Babington presented ribbons to recipients of decorations in the recent operations.	
			Military Medals to Sgt Tunstall W Sgt Corcoran M. Cpl Ryan W. Pte Crutlow M. Pte Parker R. Pte Swann P.W.	AB

A6945 Wt. W11422/M1160 350,000 12/16 D. D. & L. Forms/C.2118/14.

Army Form C. 2118.

WAR DIARY
or
INTELLIGENCE SUMMARY.
(Erase heading not required.)

Instructions regarding War Diaries and Intelligence Summaries are contained in F. S. Regs., Part II. and the Staff Manual respectively. Title pages will be prepared in manuscript.

Place	Date	Hour	Summary of Events and Information	Remarks and references to Appendices
THIEUSHOUR	JUNE 1917 28		Lt Col Lew R Manners rejoined from leave. Morning - Specialist & Company training A & B Coy on 30yds range	
			Afternoon - Inspection by G.O.C. & marching at 2.30 pm	1/AD
	29		Company & Specialist training C & D Coy on 30yds range	
	30		Paraded from THIEUSHOUR at 5.25 a.m. and marched to MICMAC	Appx B
			CAMP arriving at 12.20 p.m. Rain all day. Capt R. Lincoln returned from Leave.	1/AD
			R Manners Lt Col	
			Commanding 10th N.C.	
			1. 7. 17	

SECRET   COPY No. ......

BATTALION OPERATION ORDER No. 137.

1. The Battalion will move to Railway Dugouts to-night, 6th June, relieving the 8th Battalion YORKSHIRE REGIMENT.

2. Companies will pass the starting point, H. 17. d. 9. 2. in the order H. Q., "A", "B", "C", "D", at 10-25 p.m. Formation by platoons at 80 yards distance.

3. Route. H. 16. d. 1. 1. — KRUISSTRAAT — BRIDGE 14 — RAILWAY.

4. All baggage for return to the Quartermaster Stores, will be stacked on the road by Battalion Headquarter Mess by 9-0 p.m. No transport will be available for the line.

5. Advance parties consisting of 1 Officer and 4 N. C. O's per Company and 1 Officer and 2 N. C. O's per Headquarters, will proceed at once to take over. Parties will rendezvous at RAILWAY DUGOUTS at 5-0 p.m.

6. Dress. — Fighting Order. Greatcoats will be stacked in section bundles, in accordance with para. 4.

7. Water bottles must be filled. Companies will fill from water carts at the following times :—
    "A" and "B" Companies.   —   7-30 p.m.
    "C" and "D" Companies.   —   8-0 p.m.

8. Tools, sandbags and grenades, as laid down in Battalion Instructions No. G. I. 2, dated the 24th inst, will be issued from the forward dump at RAILWAY DUGOUTS.

9. Attention is called to Section XXXI and XXXII of " Instructions for the Training of Divisions in Offensive Action" as regards descriptive marks to be worn. Specialists descriptive marks will be issued this afternoon.

10. Completion of moves will be reported to Battalion Headquarters, RAILWAY DUGOUTS.

11. ACKNOWLEDGE.

George ......
Captain and Adjutant.

Copy No. 1. "A" Company.
"   " 2. "B"   "
"   " 3. "C"   "
"   " 4. "D"   "
"   " 5. Transport Officer.
"   " 6. Quartermaster.
"   " 7. C. O.
"   " 8. Headquarters.
"   " 9. Office.
"   " 10. War Diary.

6th June. 1917.

REPORT ON OPERATIONS FROM 6th TO THE 9th JUNE. 1917.

The Battalion left "P" Camp at 10-45 p.m. and marched to RAILWAY DUGOUTS via KRUISSTRAAT, becoming one of the two Reserve Battalions of the 23rd Division. On the march up, the Battalion came under shell fire in the vicinity of BELGIAN CHATEAU, where some heavy batteries were being engaged by hostile H. V. guns. One shell burst on the road causing several casualties in "A" Company. The Battalion was reported present in RAILWAY DUGOUTS at 1-30 a.m. on the 7th June.

Bombs, S. A. A. flares etc, had been issued to Companies by 3-0 a.m. At 3-10 a.m. two mines were exploded and a bombardment commenced. The Battalion remained in RAILWAY DUGOUTS until 11-0 a.m. when orders were received to send 2 Companies to support the 70th Brigade. "B" and "C" Companies commenced to move about 11-30 a.m. and carried bombs from ZILLEBEKE to the front line. At 1-0 p.m. orders were received for the Battalion Headquarters and remaining two Companies to move up to MONT SORREL Dugouts, and at 1-30 p.m. the move commenced. As in the case of "B" and "C" Companies, the remainder of the Battalion called at ZILLEBEKE DUMP for wire, and carried this up to our old front line. It was very hot and carrying proved a difficult task, several men collapsing under the strain. On moving up ZILLEBEKE STREET TRENCH it was found "B" and "C" Companies had been delayed and were only just then nearing their destination, and it was not until about 3-0 p.m. that Companies were in position. "B" Company came under the orders of the O. C. 11th Battalion Sherwood Foresters, and " C" Company under the orders of the O. C. 8th Battalion York and Lancs, and were to be used by them in case of emergency. Headquarters, "A" and "D" Companies moved to MONT SORREL and HEDGE STREET Dugouts in Support of the 70th Infantry Brigade. Shortly after arrival in these positions "A" Company was handed over to the O. C. 11th Sherwood Foresters and "D" Company to the O. C. 8th York and Lancs, and were disposed according to instructions of these two Commanders. Dispositions of the Battalion at 9-0 p.m. were as follows :-

"A" Company holding line from ST PETER STREET to DAVIDSON STREET.
"B" Company holding original front line about STUART STREET I. 30. b. 1. 2., I. 30. b. 4. 3. in ILLUSIVE TRENCH.
"C" Company. 2 Platoons about IMAGE CRESCENT and IMAGE AVENUE and 2 Platoons in Support in CANADA STREET and MONT SORREL, at the same time occupying a Strong Point in KLEIN ZILLEBEKE in front of the captured line.
"D" Company. 3 Platoons in MONT SORREL dugouts. 1 Platoon in IMMEDIATE TRENCH.

Companies spent all night in consolidating the positions specified above. Details of "A" and " B" Companies employed digging a trench from Sap G. to the O. G. 1. Slight alterations were made in the above dispositions during the night under the orders of the Battalion Commanders to whom Companies were lent. During the morning of the 8th, one Platoon of "B" Company under the command of 2nd Lt. J. MURPHY, which had been holding a portion of ILLUSIVE TRENCH, withdrew to our original front line. This left the Battalion with only a few details of "C" and "D" Companies in the advanced positions, the remainder were in close support. On the evening of the 8th at about 6-0 p.m. the 70th Brigade issued orders to Battalion Headquarters and two Companies to move back to the BUND, these orders were shortly afterwards cancelled and the Battalion moved to MAPLE Trench with Headquarters in RUDKIN HOUSE. The Battalion, less "A" and "B" Companies commenced to move at 10-30 p.m. but owing to "B" Company being employed on a working party, the move was not completed until 4-30 a.m. on the 9th. Headquarters and Companies were in a very congested state in the trench and were shelled during the morning by guns firing from HOOGE direction, fortunately there were no casualties. "A" and "D" Companies up to this time were still under command of the O. C. 11th Sherwood Foresters and O. C. 8th York and Lancs respectively and had been employed in consolidating during the night under very heavy shell fire. During the afternoon of the 9th, advance parties of the 24th Division came up to take over, and during the evening Battalion Headquarters, "A", "B" and "C" Companies moved out, our positions being taken over by the 8th Royal West Kents on the morning of the 10th. "D" Company was retained by the O. C. of the 8th York and Lancs until almost dawn on the 10th. The Battalion moved to "P" Camp and it arrived in by 4-30 a.m. on the 10th.

During the time the Battalion took part in the operations the casualties were as follows :-

    1 Killed.
  35 Wounded.
    1 Gassed.
  12 Missing.

2 Germans were captured in the wood behind IMAGE CRESCENT on the morning of the 8th by "C" Company.

The behaviour of the men under these trying conditions and heavy shell fire on certain occasions was extremely good.

The conduct of the runners and stretcher bearers was excellent and very conspicuous.

SECRET   COPY N0: 6

BATTALION OPERATION ORDER N0: 131.

1. The Battalion will move to DICKEBUSCH to-day and will bivouac at
   H. 34. a. 1. 8.

2. Companies will pass the starting point, Battalion Headquarters, at the
   following times :-

        Headquarter Company.   -   6-0 p.m.
        "D" Company.   -   6-2 p.m.
        "A" Company.   -   6-6 p.m.
        "B" Company.   -   6-10 p.m.
        "C" Company.   -   6-14 p.m.

   Formation.   An interval of 50 yards between platoons will be
                maintained throughout the march.

   Route.   G. 24. c. Central - G. 30. b. 1. 9. - G. 30. c. 4. 9. -
             G. 30. d. - H. 32. a. 3. 1. - H. 32. b. 8. 5. - H. 33. c. 3. 8.
             8.

3. A L. G. S. Wagon will be placed at the disposal of each Company for
   conveyance of kit. For Battalion Headquarters and Company, Mess Cart
   and 2 L. G. S. wagons. For Medical Officer Maltese Cart.
   2 L. G. S wagons for Lewis Guns already loaded, will proceed with the
   column.
   All baggage and stores must be packed outside the guard tent by 5-0 p.m.

4. Advance party to pitch the camp has already proceeded.

5. 2nd Lt. T. F. SCRIPPS will hand over this camp to the representative of
   the incoming Unit (11th West Yorks Regiment.) at 5-0 p.m.

6. Officers chargers will be at Headquarters at 6-0 p.m.

7. ACKNOWLEDGE.

                                        ....
                                             Captain and Adjutant.
                                        10th Battalion Northumberland Fusiliers.

Copy No: 1 - 4.   O's C. Companies.
  "   " 5.   Transport Officer.
  "   " 6.   Quartermaster.
  "   " 7 - 10.   Headquarters.
  "   " 11.   Office.
  "   " 12.   War Diary.

12th June. 1917.

SECRET

COPY NO. 9

BATTALION OPERATION ORDER NO. 132.

1. The Battalion will be relieved by the 12th Battalion Durham Light Infantry and one Company of the 11th N. F. to-morrow. 21st inst.

2. The 12th Battalion Durham Light Infantry will take over working parties from 10th Battalion Northumberland Fusiliers for A. D. Signals. Xth Corps.

3. Advance parties consisting of 2nd Lt. L. W. Mather and 4 N. C. O's per Company (1 per Platoon) will be at HELLBLAST CORNER at 11-0 a.m. sharp.

4. Guides. One guide per Company and Headquarters will be at HELLBLAST CORNER at 11-0 a.m. to guide Advance parties into their billets. Officers Commanding Companies will be responsible that guides are at HELLBLAST CORNER at 5-45 p.m. to guide Companies into their billets.

5. On relief Companies will move off in the order H. Q. "D", "C", "B", and "A" to HELLBLAST CORNER, where they will take lorries vacated by 12th Battalion Durham Light Infantry.

6. O. C. "B" Company will detail 1 Officer to be at HELLBLAST CORNER to meet 12th Battalion Durham Light Infantry and to superintend lorries until the Battalion turn up. He will also note the number of men carried by each lorry.

7. Transport. Transport will proceed by road. Arrangements for Officers' kits will be notified later.

8. ACKNOWLEDGE.

.... Captain.
O. C. 10th Battalion Northumberland Fusiliers.

```
Copy No. 1.  "A" Company.
  "    "  2.  "B"    "
  "    "  3.  "C"    "
  "    "  4.  "D"    "
  "    "  5.  Transport Officer.
  "    "  6.  Quartermaster.
  "    "  7 - 8. Headquarters.
  "    "  9.  Office.
  "    "  10. War Diary.
```

20th June. 1917.

App B

SECRET   COPY NO......

PRELIMINARY BATTALION OPERATION ORDER NO. 132.

1. The Brigade will move to MICMAC CAMP on the 30th inst.

2. Advance party composed of 2nd Lt. H. F. Knowles and 1 N. C. O. per Company, will proceed to take over to-morrow. They will report at Brigade Headquarters at 10-0 a.m. to-morrow, 29th inst.

3. Receipts for all material taken over must be sent into the Orderly Room by 12-0 noon 30th inst.

4. 2nd Lt. H. F. W. Knowles may take his kit but not his servant.

5. Transport Officer will arrange for half limber to collect 2nd Lt. H. F. W. Knowles's kit from "B" Company at 9-30 a.m. and deliver it to Brigade Headquarters by 9-50 a.m..

............................2nd Lt.
A/Adjutant.

Copy No. 1. O. C. "A" Company.
"   "   2. O. C. "B" Company.
"   "   3. O. C. "C" Company.
"   "   4. O. C. "D" Company.
"   "   5. Transport Officer.
"   "   6. Quartermaster.
"   "   7. R. S. M.
"   "   8. C. O.
"   "   9. Office.
"   " 10. File.

28th June. 1917.

S E C R E T   C O P Y   N O^o......9......

BATTALION OPERATION ORDER NO^o 133.

1. The 68th Brigade will march to MICMAC CAMP, relieving 72 nd Infantry Brigade to-morrow. 30th inst.

2. During the march, intervals of quarter mile between Battalions and 200 yards between half Battalions will be maintained.

3. The Battalion will form up on the road outside Headquarters in the order - Headquarters, "B", "A", "D", "C", ready to move off at 5-25 a.m. Head of the Column at Headquarters gate facing North.

4. 2nd Lt. P. L. Delaney will be responsible for direction.

5. Transport will march with the Battalion and will form up in rear of "C" Company ready to move off with the Battalion at 5-25 a.m. except baggage wagons, which will proceed to square GODEWAERSVELDE and will march from there under orders of O. C. 91st Company A. S. C. at 7-0 a.m.

6. All stores and Officers Kits for conveyance by Motor Lorry, will be stacked by the gate at each camp by 5.0 a.m. and one man left in charge from each Company and Headquarters.

7. One man of Headquarters will also be left behind to meet the baggage lorry at Brigade Headquarters at 6-0 a.m. and guide it to this camp. The lorries will not leave this area before 8-0 a.m.

8. Steel Helmets to be stacked at Q. M. Stores by 6-0 p.m. to-night.

9. All water bottles to be filled to-night and inspected by Company Officers in the morning.

10. Strictest march discipline will be maintained. Halts will be made at 10 minutes before each clock hour and the march resumed at the clock hour. Numbers of men falling out will be reported to Orderly Room immediately on arrival in Camp.

11. ACKNOWLEDGE.

                                                                   Langley Davies
                                                    ....2nd Lt.
                                                                        A/Adjutant.

Copy No^o 1.   "A" Company.
"   "   2.   "B" Company.
"   "   3.   "C" Company.
"   "   4.   "D" Company.
"   "   5.   Transport Officer.
"   "   6.   Quartermaster.
"   "   7.   R. S. M.
"   "   8.   C. O.
"   "   9.   Office.
"   "   10. File.

29th June. 1917.

10 NF Vol 23

WAR DIARY or INTELLIGENCE SUMMARY

Army Form C. 2118.

Place	Date	Hour	Summary of Events and Information	Remarks and references to Appendices
MICMAC CAMP	JULY 1917 1st		Fighting Strength. 34. 852. Away from Unit 11. 117. Ration Strength 24. 738. Trench Strength 23. 658. O. OR. Church of England Parade 11.15 a.m. Transport removed to Camp 13. The neighbourhood was shelled at intervals during the day.	
do	2	1.30p	Enemy commenced shelling again - some damage being done to adjacent camp. Morning Bayonet fighting practice under Brigade Instructor. Major G.F. Ashton M.C. reported for duty, after undergoing a C.O.'s Course in England, and took over duties of 2nd in Command of the Battalion. Draft of 117 O.R. arrived and was taken on the strength.	
do	3		Morning. Inspection of Gas Helmets by the Divisional Gas Officer, followed by Rifle drill etc. New draft of 117 O.R. was inspected by the Brigadier General, and later by the O.C. Battalion.	23 C
do	4		Visit of H.M. the King. Battalion turned out on outward & homeward journey to welcome His Majesty. Battn at RENINGHELST.	

Army Form C. 2118.

WAR DIARY
or
INTELLIGENCE SUMMARY.
(Erase heading not required.)

Instructions regarding War Diaries and Intelligence Summaries are contained in F.S. Regs., Part II. and the Staff Manual respectively. Title pages will be prepared in manuscript.

Place	Date	Hour	Summary of Events and Information	Remarks and references to Appendices
MICMAC CAMP	JULY 4		Bayonet fighting practices under the Brigade Instructor. Coy Commanders and Specialists made a reconnaissance of MOUNT SORREL SECTOR. A F.G.C.M. was held at Batalion H.Q. under the Presidency of Major L.I. Ashton M.C. for the trial of :- 3712 Pte Bland T. charged with absence from 30.5.17 until 1.6.17, and 46580 Pte Davison L.I. charged with self inflicted wound — both of this Batalion. Pte. Davison was found "Not Guilty and discharged.	
	5		Officers attended at Bde. H.Q. to meet L.O.C. Division who explained the nature of the work to be carried out by the Batalion while in the line. The L.G.S.O. afterwards decorated 19617 Cpl. N. Bell with the D.C.M. medal ribbon. Batalion paraded at 9.30pm moved to the MOUNT SORREL SECTOR Coy. "A" Men were now being made and "A" Coy produced 3 casualties — one killed + 2 wounded. Relief completed about 2 a.m.	
MOUNT SORREL SECTOR	6		Enemy artillery very active all day. Working parts of 7 Officers + 300 O.R. was provided. Considerable enemy bombardment from about 11-30 pm	

WAR DIARY
or
INTELLIGENCE SUMMARY.
(Erase heading not required.)

Army Form C. 2118.

Place	Date	Hour	Summary of Events and Information	Remarks and references to Appendices
MOUNT SORREL SECTOR	6		to 2.30 a.m. but notwithstanding this all ranks worked exceedingly well. Casualties:- Lieut A.L. COOK and 2nd Lieut M.L. WILKINSON and 7 O.R. wounded.	
	7		Enemy artillery much quieter. A few whizz bangs were dropped near METROPOLITAN LEFT during the afternoon, and about 6 p.m. this area was shelled with H.E. shrapnel. No damage was done to our trenches. About 6 p.m. a number of our own and enemy aeroplanes flew over our lines and shortly afterwards was observed to come down in flames behind our lines. At 7.10 p.m. another plane came down within the precincts of ZILLEBEKE but it is not known whether these were our own or enemy machine. Working party of 6 Officers and 250 O.R. applied according to Bde. orders unfortunately quite night unsuccessful, and there were no casualties.	
MOUNT SORREL SECTOR	8		Casualties:- Nil. 2nd Lt M. Wilkinson died of wounds at 17 C.C.S. at 8.20 P.M. Working parties according to Bde. programme. Intelligence:- Enemy was very quiet during the night. Working parties 6 Officers & 250 O.R.	

WAR DIARY
or
INTELLIGENCE SUMMARY.
(Erase heading not required.)

Army Form C. 2118.

Place	Date	Hour	Summary of Events and Information	Remarks and references to Appendices
MOUNT SORREL SECTOR	9		The Battalion relieved the 11th NF's in the FRONT LINE MOUNT SORREL SECTOR. Relief was completed by 11.30am 10.7.17. Casualties NIL. Working parties 2 Officers 60 ORs according to Bde Programme. Intelligence during relief. The enemy fired Machine guns and rifle grenades at Nos. 3 and 4 of Left Coy at 10 mnt intervals. Sgt Steel and Pte Oins Im were slightly wounded during relief.	A/A "B"
MOUNT SORREL SECTOR	10		Casualties Sgt Steel and Pte Oins Im. Machine gun fire reported by rifle grenades and Lithgams F Goh was heavy shelled between Wadrug of 6 PM and then 11.7.17. Patrols sent out at 11.40 PM from 1.30 to T.5.80. The Patrol consisted of one Officer and two ORs. ORs 2 patrol one Officer and two ORs went towards I.30.r.95.80 an enemy the Patrol moved down the front. The enemy opened out with an R.M.Gy Barrage on I.3a.N(70.80)(70.45) and (90.30)(90.40) they were	

WAR DIARY
or
INTELLIGENCE SUMMARY.
(Erase heading not required.)

Army Form C. 2118.

Place	Date	Hour	Summary of Events and Information	Remarks and references to Appendices
MOUNT SORREL SECTOR	10		made to advance at this point the enemy fired at patrol with 40 rifle grenades. The Patrol returned to our lines at 1.30am. near Hagebeard Alley 1 1/4 D LANE was strongly held. Working parties 190 O.R.s 3 hours returning. IMAGE and ILLUSIVE SUPPT. digging new trench at I.30.d (70.75)(63.70). Relieving old front line "A" Coy relieved "B" Coy in Right FRONT LINE. "D" Coy relieved "C" Coy in LEFT FRONT LINE. Casualties during relief. CHIMIDGELEY and Pre. TALLSOPP killed & 4 men wounded and 2 missing. Intelligence. Enemy was very quiet after relief. A patrol of 1 offr. and 2 O.R.s went out from advance control "Right" Coy and proceeded down ILLUSIVE DRIVE. Nothing was seen of the enemy. Patrol returned at 1.30am. 12in. Working parties 2 Officers & Quick working parties of 11 N.E.s and have thrown 20m 3 horse hurling out new entanglement. F.S.O.	
MOUNT SORREL SECTOR	11			

WAR DIARY
or
INTELLIGENCE SUMMARY

Army Form C. 2118.

Place	Date	Hour	Summary of Events and Information	Remarks and references to Appendices
MOUNT SORREL SECTOR	12		Casualties 4 men killed and 3 wounded. One outpost Junction of LEFT Coy & Intelligence IMAGE SUPPT was shelled by 5.9 and 4.2" during the night. At 11.15PM enemy fired a golden rain rocket from ILIAD LANE and this artillery opened on Sap "J". During night enemy was very active supporting the Junction of "J" Sap and old British Front line. I.30 & 30.65. Working parties 60 ORs 3 hours reclaiming IMAGE SUPPT. Carrying party to front line coy, erecting temporary cookhouse.	
MOUNT SORREL SECTOR	13		Enemy aeroplane very active over our lines, supposed to be taking photographs. Two patrols went out — (1) took up positions at (1) I.25.a.05.40 (2) I.25.a.12.20. On approaching these posts they were fired on and the enemy was found to be holding these posts. Casualties 1 officer (commanding officer) wounded Lt. Col R.W.Barnes C.M.G, D.S.O, 3 ORs (accidental)	

# WAR DIARY or INTELLIGENCE SUMMARY

Army Form C. 2118.

Place	Date	Hour	Summary of Events and Information	Remarks and references to Appendices
MOUNT SORREL SECTOR	13		Working parties 20 men 3 hour putting out wire Entanglement 60 men 3 hour infantry outpost position and "F" Sap. The Battalion was relieved by the 9th YORKS and proceeded to MICMAC CAMP. arriving there about 4.30 a.m.	App "C"
MICMAC CAMP.	14		Coys bathed. Major J.J. Ashton M.C. assumed command of the Battalion vice Lt. Col. Lord R.W.O. Manners D.S.O. C.M.G. wounded.	
do	15		Sunday - Usual Church Parade.	
	16		Working party of 1 Officer + 50 O.R. provided for work under 178th Tunnelling Coy at SPOIL BANK. Company parades according to programme of work issued.	
	17		Working party of 1 Officer + 50 O.R. to work with 178th Tunnelling Coy. Baths at RENINGHELST. Coy parades as per programme.	
	18		Working party as above and parade in accordance with programme. Draft of 11 O.R. arrived and posted to "A" + "B" Coys. 2nd Lieut C.E. OATES reported for duty & was posted to "A" Coy.	

WAR DIARY
or
INTELLIGENCE SUMMARY.
(Erase heading not required.)

Army Form C. 2118.

Place	Date	Hour	Summary of Events and Information	Remarks and references to Appendices
MICMAC CAMP	19		Working party as previous day. Work according to programme. Bath at PENINGHELST for men who had not already bathed. Lieut Col. W.H. MIDDLETON D.S.O. arrived and assumed Command of the Battalion vice Major G.L. Ashton M.C. 2nd Lieut G.L. SMITH (who went on platoon of 'C' Coy was attached to the Regt as A-DICKERSON) killed. Draft of 4 O.R. arrived. 2nd Lieut W. STEWART and T. NISBITT reporting for duty. Parade as per programme. Fatigue party of 1 officer + 39 O.R.	
	20		Paraded for work at Div. Bomb Store.	
	21		Battalion proceeded by march route to THIEUSHOOK - arriving at mid-day.	App. D
THIEUSHOOK	22		Church Parade. Major G.F. ASHTON M.C. granted leave to England.	
	23		Parade as per programme. Draft of 23 O.R. arrived.	
	24		Battalion was inspected by L/O.C. in full ceremonial 'D' Coy. Dress: Battle Order. Ad. L.O.C. afterwards addressed all officers.	
	25		Work according to programme. 2nd Lieut MARTIN D. MOORE E. PEARSON I.W.	

WAR DIARY
INTELLIGENCE SUMMARY
(Erase heading not required.)

Army Form C. 2118.

Place	Date	Hour	Summary of Events and Information	Remarks and references to Appendices
THIEDSHOCK	26		Parades according to programme. One section programme of work was carried out by the Artillery in the afternoon and an invitation was issued to the Battalion to take part in same.	
	27		Parades as per programme. A + B Coy on the Range at R. 23.a. 9 2nd Lieut Jnr. GIBB arrived for duty & 2nd Lieut L.W. MATHER attached to the strength - transferred to R.F.C.	
	28		Training as per programme. A Lecture on "Discipline in the field" was given by the D.A.A.G. 23rd Division at Bde H.Q. at (?)noon - Company Commanders with Adjutant attending Brigade Sports were held in the afternoon.	
	29		Church parades.	
	30		The Battalion moved by train from CHESTRE to ST OMER and hence by march to SETQUES. Billets in various farms etc in the village.	App E
	31		Programme of work arranged could not be carried out owing to rain, indoor instructional work carried on both morning and afternoon.	

M.W.W.D. Lieut. Col.
Commanding 10th North'd Fus.

S E C R E T.   C O P Y N O. 11

                    App. A.

                    BATTALION OPERATION ORDER NO. 134.
                    ─────────────────────────────────

1. The Battalion will move into Support position MONT SORREL SECTOR on the night of 5/6th instant.

2. Dispositions will be as follows :-

   "A" Company.   METROPOLITAN LEFT.
   "B" Company.   CANADA STREET TUNNELS.
   "C" Company.   SEBA TUNNELS.
                          1 Lewis gun at junction of WINNIPEG STREET AND ST. PETERS STREET.

   "D" Company.   RUDKIN HOUSE.
   Battn. H.Q.   SEBA TUNNELS.

3. ORDER OF MARCH. H.Q. "B", "C", "D" and "A".   Battalion will parade ready to march from Camp at 9.30 p.m.

4. ROUTE.   Overland to DICKIBUSCH - CAFE BELGE - DERBY RD. (Corduroy Road) (~~Corner~~) SHRAPNEL CORNER - VALLEY COTTAGES.
   "A" Coy. route selected by O.C. Company as far as point to meet guides.

5. At least 100 yards interval will be maintained between platoons.

6. Guides for "A" Company will be at junction/VERBRANDON ROAD and PANAMA CANAL. "B", "C", "D" Companies and Battalion H.Q. at VALLEY COTTAGES.

7. Advance Parties of 1 Officer and 4 N.C.O's per Company and 2 N.C.O's from H.Q. will proceed to take over tomorrow morning leaving Camp at 9 a.m.

8. All trench-stores, air-photos, maps, defence schemes and petrol tins will be taken over, and receipts for same exchanged. These receipts to be sent in to Orderly Room by 12 noon 6th instant.

9. COOKING. Tea only can be made. All meat will be sent up ready cooked. Only one Cook per Company will proceed to the line, the remainder will stay with the cookers to prepare the meat.

10. WATER.   "A", "B" and "C" Companies can obtain water in their Company areas. "D" Company will draw from MAPLE COPSE.

11. RATION DUMPS.   "A" Company   -   LONE TREE DUMP.
                    "B", "C", "D" and H.Q. - On the road half-way between VALLEY COTTAGES AND RUDKIN HOUSE.

12. BAGGAGE.   Baggage will be stacked as follows :-

    For the line   - Opposite H.Q. in the avenue of trees by 8 p.m.
    For return to store - Brick building at road end of avenue of trees by 8 p.m.

13. LEWIS GUNS and ammunition - Stacked with baggage for the line by 8 p.m. Guards to be left with Lewis Guns and baggage and these men will proceed to the line with the limbers.

14. TRANSPORT.   1 Limber for Companies.
                 Mess Cart and ½ limber for Headquarters.
                 Maltese Cart for M.O.
                 1 Lewis Gun limber for "B", "C" and "D" guns.
                 ½ "   "   "   "   "A" Company guns.
    "A" Company ½ Limber to go to LONE TREE DUMP.

BATTALION OPERATION ORDER NO. 134 Contd.

15. The following guards will be sent to report to Headquarters, 70th Infantry Brigade, at LARCH WOOD at 3 p.m. tomorrow :-

   1. "A" Company.1 N.C.O. and 4 men for water Guard at I.29.b.2.7.
   2. "D" Company.1 N.C.O. and 3 men for guard on iron rations at VALLEY COTTAGES.
   3. "D" Company.1 N.C.O. and 3 men for water guard at I.22.d.90.05.

16. Completion of reliefs to be reported in code.

17. ACKNOWLEDGE.

                                                 ....2/Lt. A/Adjt.
                             10th Battalion. Northumberland Fusiliers.

4th July 1917.

```
Copy No. 1 to O.C. "A" Coy.
  "   "  2  "  O.C. "B" Coy.
  "   "  3  "  O.C. "C" Coy.
  "   "  4  "  O.C. "D" Coy.
  "   "  5  "  Transport Officer.
  "   "  6  "  Quartermaster.
  "   "  7  "  Commanding Officer.
  "   "  8  "  2nd. in Command.
  "   "  9  "  Adjutant.
  "   " 10  "  Office.
  "   " 11  "  War Diary.
  "   " 12  "  Regtl. Sergt. Major.
```

SECRET   No......
                                         App. B.

Operation Order No. 135.

1. The Battalion will relieve the 11th N.F. tomorrow night 9th/10th inst. commencing 10.30 p.m.

2. Dispositions
   "C" Coy relieve "D" Coy 11th N.F. left front line. H.Q. HEDGE ST. TUNNEL.
   "B" Coy relieve "B" Coy 11th N.F. right front line. H.Q. IMAGE RES. I.30.d.15.90
   "A" Coy relieve "A" Coy 11th N.F. Support H.Q. CANADA STREET. TUN.
   "D" Coy relieve "C" Coy 11th N.F. RESERVE H.Q. HEDGE ST. TUNNEL.
   Battn H.Q. & R.A.P. HEDGE ST.

3. O.C. Coys will make their own arrangements with O.C. Coys they are to relieve about advance parties, taking over guides etc.

4. Signed receipts for stores, defence schemes, maps etc handed and taken over to reach this office by 10 a.m. 10th inst.

5. Ration Dump at Valley Cottages.
   'A' Coy will carry for 'B' Coy
   'D' Coy   "   "   " 'C' Coy

6. 11th N.F. will relieve the detached guards of A & D Coys tomorrow after and on relief guards will rejoin their Coys.

7. An extra days rations will be issued to B & C Coys tonight and these will be held in reserve in case of

emergency.

All men coming from the front line Coys must bring down an empty water tin and men going up take a full one.

9. Completion of relief to be reported in code.

10. Acknowledge.

8/4/19

J. Langton
Lieut & Adjt
10th North'd Fus.

Copies to
   O.C A Coy
   O.C B Coy
   O.C D Coy
   O.C C Coy.

S E C R E T.   C O P Y   NO: ....

BATTALION OPERATION ORDER NO' 13. B.   App. C.

1. The Battalion will be relieved by the 9th Yorks on the night of the 13/14th inst.

2. On relief the Battalion will proceed to MICMAC CAMP.

3. Advance party consisting of 2nd Lt. P. L. Delaney and 1 N. C. O. per Company and Headquarters, will proceed on the morning of the 13th inst to take over the camp vacated by the 9th YORKS. Party will rendezvous at MICMAC CAMP at 12-0 noon.

4. All stores, maps, defence schemes, schemes of work, aeroplane photographs etc will be handed over and receipts obtained. These will be forwarded to O. R. by 12-0 noon on the 14th inst.

5. Signed lists of stores taken over at Camp will be rendered at the same time.

6. Baggage will be stacked at Battalion Ration Dump by 10-0 p.m.

7. Transport will be provided as follows :-

        1 Limber for Companies.
        Mess Cart for Headquarters.
        2 L. G. Limbers for guns after they are relieved.

8. Guides for incoming Unit will be provided as follows :-

Right Front Company.	1 per Platoon. Company H. Q. RUDKIN HOUSE 10-0 p.m.
Left Front Company.	1 per Platoon. Company H. Q. SEBA TUNNELS. 10-0 p.m.
Support Position.	1 per Platoon at Junction VERBRANDEN ROAD and PANAMA CANAL. 10-30 p.m.
Reserve Position.	DO DO
H. Q.	1 N. C. O., RUDKIN HOUSE. 10-0 p.m.

O. C. Companies will ensure that guides are familiar with the routes from the rendezvous by night.
2nd Lt. SWINDELL will be in charge of the guides at the rendezvous.

9. Completion of relief to be reported by runner to Battalion H. Q.

10. ACKNOWLEDGE.

                                       (Sgd) E. G. BODGER. 2nd Lt.
                                              A/Adjutant.

Copy. No' 1. "A" Company.
   "   "   2. "B" Company.
   "   "   3. "C" Company.
   "   "   4. "D" Company.
   "   "   5. Transport Officer.
   "   "   6. 2nd in Command & Transport.
   "   "   7. Quartermaster.
   "   "   8. Office.

SECRET.   COPY No:........

10th BATTALION NORTHUMBERLAND FUSILIERS.
OPERATION ORDER No: 137.

App. D

Reference Sheets 27 and 28.

Scale. 1/40,000.

1. The Battalion will proceed by march route to THIEUSHOOK (Q.30.a.1.1.) on the 21st July. 1917.

2. Route – LACLYTTE – WESTOUTRE – BERTHEN.   2nd Lt. L. W. Mather will be responsible for direction.

3. The Battalion will parade at 7-30 a.m. on the ground in front of H. Q. and will be at the starting point (X roads N. 2. c. 2½. 2.) at 8-0 a.m.

4. Order of March. :- Headquarters, "A", "B", "C" and "D" Companies. The Band will parade with the Battalion.

5. Transport will march with the Battalion.

6. An interval of 200 yards between Companies and 400 yards between Battalions and other Units will be kept, and the strictest march discipline will be maintained. The number of men falling out on the march will be reported to Orderly Room on arrival at destination.

7. There will be a half hour halt at 9-50 a.m. besides the usual 10 minutes halt.

8. All kit, stores etc, will be stacked outside Quartermaster Stores, by 7-0 a.m. One Officer's servant per Company and Headquarters will be detailed to accompany kits etc. One lorry will be available.

9. Water bottles will be filled before leaving.

10. Breakfast will be at 6-30 a.m. and dinners will be served on arrival at Camp.

11. A rear party consisting of 1 Sergeant and 2. O. R. will remain to hand over the camp and stores to incoming Unit. This party will be detailed by O. C. "A" Company, and should report to Orderly Room at 7-15 a.m. for instructions.

12. O's C. Companies will see that all huts and lines are left in a clean condition.

13. ACKNOWLEDGE.

.................................2nd Lt.
A/Adjutant. 10th Battalion Northumberland Fusiliers.

```
Copy. No' 1. "A" Company.
  "    "  2. "B" Company.
  "    "  3. "C" Company.
  "    "  4. "D" Company.
  "    "  5. Transport Officer.
  "    "  6. Quartermaster.
  "    "  7. C. O.
  "    "  8. R. S. M.
  "    "  9. War Diary.
  "    " 10. Office.
```

20th July. 1917.

SECRET   COPY NO'..........

BATTALION OPERATION ORDER NO' 156.

App. E.

1. Battalion will move by train to-morrow from CAESTRE to ST OMER, and thence by march to SETQUES.

2. Battalion will fall in on the road, head of column at gate of "D" Company's field, ready to move off at 10-45 a.m.   Order :- H. Q., "D", "C", "B", "A".

3. Advance party consisting of 2nd Lt. D. L. Hutchinson and 1 O. R. per Company and Headquarters, will report to Brigade Headquarters at 8-0 a.m. to-morrow.

4. 2nd Lt. J. MURPHY will report to Lt. GREEN at CAESTRE station at 11-45 a.m. with "entraining state" which he will receive from Orderly Room before proceeding.

5. All baggage, including camp kettles, will be stacked on the road outside each billet by 9-30 a.m.   Only 2 O. R. including 1 cook per Company and Headquarters, will go on the lorries.

6. Men must carry on them, rations and water for consumption on the journey.

7. ACKNOWLEDGE.

                                                    Hanefey Davis
                                                  ....2nd Lt.
          A/Adjutant. 10th Battalion Northumberland Fusiliers.

```
Copy No' 1.   "A" Company.
   "    "  2.   "B" Company.
   "    "  3.   "C" Company.
   "    "  4.   "D" Company.
   "    "  5.   Transport Officer.
   "    "  6.   Quartermaster.
   "    "  7.   C. O.
   "    "  8.   R. S. M.
   "    "  9.   War Diary.
   "    " 10.   Office.
```

29th July. 1917.

WAR DIARY
or
INTELLIGENCE SUMMARY.

(Erase heading not required.)

Army Form C. 2118.

10 N F

Oct 24 1917

Place	Date	Hour	Summary of Events and Information	Remarks and references to Appendices
FOVES.	AUGUST 1		Fighting Strength 38.937 Away from Unit 9.200. Ration Strength C.O.R. 28.740. Trench Strength 26.660. Programme of work carried out pretty undisturbed with being too wet in morning and afternoon. Weather: Indoor instructional work done. 2nd Lieut H.G. STEELE reported for duty. I assumed command of "A" Coy.	C.O.R.
	2		Parades on per Programme - made rifle pull test	
	3		Route march arranged for the 4th Coys was cancelled - Officers & Platoon Sgts having to assemble too-early for leaving by day-light - men weaker any had.	
	4		Parades according to programme. Kit inspection by M.O. The following Officers reported their arrival and were taken on strength of Battalion and posted to Coys as follows:- 2nd Lieut ALLAN E. "A" Coy 2nd Lieut CARR "B" Coy. 2nd Lieut BOOTH H.G.B. "B" Coy. 2nd Lieut DOW W.O. "C" Coy. 2nd Lieut BAKER J.C. "C" Coy	
	5		Church parades	
	6		"A" & "D" Coys on the range at P.35.c. from 9am - 11am. "B" & "C" Coys from 1pm - 5pm. Lewis Gunners fired 5am to finish	

Army Form C. 2118.

WAR DIARY
or
INTELLIGENCE SUMMARY.
(Erase heading not required.)

Place	Date	Hour	Summary of Events and Information	Remarks and references to Appendices
SETQUES	6		A G.C.M. was held at the Head Quarters 13th D.L.I. for the trial of N° 8714 Cpl. DICKINSON P. 10th Yorks. Regt. on a charge of being drunk. Accused was found "not guilty"	
	7		Battalion was inspected by the Army Commander at 3 pm.	
	8		Baths at ST OMER from 7 am to 1.3 pm. N.C.O's of A & B Coys paraded under Sergt. Instructor. Bayonet fighting instruction to N.C.O's of "C" & "D" at 11.30 am." in the afternoon.	
SERQUES	9		The Battalion marched to SERQUES arriving about 12 noon. Billeted in farms etc.	APP "A"
	10		Training as per programme issued. Draft of 52 O.R. arrived	
	11		D°	
	12		All Coys on Range at P.13.k.8.Q.7.a.	
	13		Morning spent in kit inspection, cleaning of arms, equipment, clothing etc. Brigade Night Operations carried on as per particulars issued. Captain E.E. DORMAN-SMITH having reported his arrival in town on the strength 11.8.17.	
	14		Coys at disposal of Coy. Commanders from 10-12 noon. Church Service parade	

WAR DIARY
or
INTELLIGENCE SUMMARY.
(Erase heading not required.)

Army Form C. 2118.

Place	Date	Hour	Summary of Events and Information	Remarks and references to Appendices
	Aug.			
EPERLECQUES	14		under M.O. for instruction.	
	15		Training as per programme. Five Officers + N.C.Os attended demonstration by Tcw Coy Officers at EPERLECQUES. 4 Officers and R.S.M. proceeded to view model (at A.30.c central - Sheet 28) of ground S.E. of POELCAPPELLE - ST JULIEN ROAD and N. of the STROOMBEEK.	
	16		Training according to programme. 5 Officers to see above model. 2STR to the 5th Army Musketry Camps.	
	17		Training as per programme. 5 Officers to view model as above.	
	18		'A' + 'B' arrange Coy training as per programme. 'B' remaining. 5 Officers to view model as above.	
	19		Church parade. C.O. + Coy Commanders reconnoitred ground for attack practice. Aquatic Sports were held on the canal in the afternoon. Lieut Col Lord R.W.O. Hannes rejoined Assumed Command	
	20		Battalion carried out a (practice) attack in conjunction with the 13th R.R.J. on the training area	
ASQUERY	21		Training as per programme. Platoon Commanders attended a demonstration	

WAR DIARY
or
INTELLIGENCE SUMMARY.
(Erase heading not required.)

Army Form C. 2118.

Place	Date	Hour	Summary of Events and Information	Remarks and references to Appendices
	Aug.			
ST DVES	21		Into method of opening hostile M.G. in an engagement.	
	22		Brigade carried out a practice attack on the Training Area.	
	23		"B" D. Coy. on the field firing Range at GUEMY. A & C Coys. as per programme of work.	App. B
			Transport moved to OUDERDOM AREA	
	24		Battalion moved to OTTAWA CAMP entraining from WATTEN to RENINGHELST, arriving at camp about 2 a.m. the following day	
OTTAWA	25		Day spent in rest cleaning up.	
CAMP.	26		Church parade at 11.30 a.m. Four Officers (including the C.O.) proceeded to reconnoitre the line.	
	27		Parade as per programme. Officers proceeded over line.	
	28		Do. Do.	
	29		Do. Battalion moved at 4.30 p.m. to Camp	
			at H. 27. d. 3. 7.	
DICKEBUSCH	30		Coys. at disposal of Coy. Commanders. Details left to man Engineers Camp. Officers & N.C.O. proceeded to view line	
	31		Do. Baths at RENINGHELST.	

J.C. Manners Lieut Col
Commanding 10th [?] Fusiliers

SECRET   COPY NO'........

BATTALION OPERATION ORDER. 139.

Reference Map. HAZEBROUCK. 5. A. and 27.a. S. E.

1. The Battalion will march to SERQUES to-morrow. 9th inst.

2. The Battalion including Transport will parade on the top road, head of the column opposite "D" Company's Mess, ready to move off at 8-0 a.m. Order of March. - H. Q. "C"., "D", Band, "A", "B" Transport. 200 yards interval will be maintained between Companies and Transport. The strictest march discipline will be maintained. The numbers of men falling out on the march will be reported to Battalion Headquarters on arrival in billets.

3. All kit will be stacked at Company Headquarters by 7-30 a.m. Each Company Headquarters, + Q. M. will each leave two men for the purposes of loading.

4. 2nd Lt. J. C. RAY, will remain behind, and after the motor lorry is loaded he will collect the men mentioned in para. 3, and will march them to SERQUES.

5. At W. 4. a. 8. 5. all Transport will take the road to the west to ZUDAUSQUES and will halt with the head of the column at W. 3. a. 8. 5. until the 11th N. F. have passed. They will follow the 11th N. F.

6. ACKNOWLEDGE.

.............................2nd Lt.
A/Adjutant. 10th Battalion Northumberland Fusiliers.

```
Copy. No' 1.    "A" Company.
 "    "  2.    "B" Company.
 "    "  3.    "C" Company.
 "    "  4.    "D" Company.
 "    "  5.    Transport Officer.
 "    "  6.    Quartermaster.
 "    "  7.    C. O.
 "    "  8.    R. S. M.
 "    "  9.    War Diary.
 "    " 10.    Office.
```

9th August. 1917.

SECRET. FILE "B"   COPY NO. 10

BATTALION OPERATION ORDER NO. 142.

1. Battalion will move to OTTAWA CAMP to-morrow, 24th inst, entraining from WATTEN to RENINGHELST, arriving at latter place 11-20 p.m.

2. Battalion will march to WATTEN. Parade ready to march off at 5-15 p.m. Head of Column to be opposite Q. M. Stores. Order :-
Headquarters, "C", "D", Band, "B", "A".

3. All kit and stores to be stacked on the road outside Company Headquarters by 8-0 a.m. Dixies will be retained and carried to the Station.

4. 2nd Lt. W. L. DOW. will report to entraining Officer Captain. E. E. DORMAN SMITH.M. G. at WATTEN Station, at 7-0 p.m. with entraining States which he will obtain at Orderly Room before leaving.

5. Company Commanders, Q. M. and R. S. M. will render Entraining States to Orderly Room by 12-0 noon.

6. After detraining at RENINGHELST an interval of 200 yards between Companies will be maintained.

7. Billet clean Certificates will be handed to 2nd in Command before moving off.

8. ACKNOWLEDGE.

.... Captain & Adjt.

Copy No. 1. "A" Company.
"   "   2. "B" Company.
"   "   3. "C" Company.
"   "   4. "D" Company.
"   "   5. Quartermaster.
"   "   6. Transport Officer.
"   "   7. C. O.
"   "   8. R. S. M.
"   "   9. War Diary.
"   " 10. Office.

23rd August, 1917.

CONFIDENTIAL.

WAR DIARY

of

10th (S) BATTALION, NORTHUMBERLAND FUSILIERS.

From.   Sept. 1st 1917.

To.   Sept. 30th 1917.

Army Form C. 2118.

WAR DIARY
or
INTELLIGENCE SUMMARY.
(Erase heading not required.)

Place	Date	Hour	Summary of Events and Information	Remarks and references to Appendices
	SEPTEMBER			
DICKEBUSCH	1		Fighting Strength R. O. OR. 46. 980 Alway from Unit 14. 170 Ration Strength R.33. 819 Trench Strength 31. 739. Bayonet parade, attack formation. 10 a.m. Practice attack for men going into Asylum.	O. OTR.
PALACE CAMP.	2		Battalion moved to PALACE CAMP (H. 25.c. 4.0) at 9.25 a.m. Voluntary Church Service in evening.	APP. A.
STEENVOORDE	3		Battalion moved by march route to the STEENVOORDE AREA at 12.57 p.m. Billeted in farms which were somewhat scattered.	APP. B
	4		Foot and rifle inspection following of billets.	
NOORDPENE AREA	5		Battalion marched to N.E. NOORDPENE AREA via OXELAERE - RAVINCOVE at 6.35 a.m. and arrived in billets about 1.30 p.m. Details from Reinforcement Camp rejoined.	APP. C
	6		Morning spent in cleaning up improving billets. Officers employed training area.	
	7		Training as per programme.	
	8		D° 4 Officers proceeded to view the line. 2nd Lieut. J.W. McGUFFOG Appointed 2nd Lieut Bombing officer to "D" Coy.	

Army Form C. 2118.

WAR DIARY
or
INTELLIGENCE SUMMARY.
(Erase heading not required.)

Instructions regarding War Diaries and Intelligence Summaries are contained in F. S. Regs., Part II. and the Staff Manual respectively. Title pages will be prepared in manuscript.

Place	Date	Hour	Summary of Events and Information	Remarks and references to Appendices
	SEPTEMBER			
NOORDPEENE	9		Training as per programme	
AREA	10		Do.	
	11		Do. Lieut Col. Lord R.W.O. MANNERS C.M.G. D.S.O.	
			Lieut Col. Lord R.W.O. MANNERS C.M.G. D.S.O.	
			Revised when reconnaitering the line. 2nd Lieu A.R. THOMPSON reported	
			On arrival was posted to "C" Coy.	
	12		Training as per programme.	
	13		The Battalion moved by march route to "STEENVOORDE" (Central) AREA at	APP. D.
			1.30 pm and arrived about 5.30 pm. Billets in Farmhouses.	
STEENVOORDE	14		Arrival of Lieut Col. R.W.O. MANNERS C.M.G. D.S.O. at BLAKE HUSCH.	
			At 8.25 am the Battalion moved by march route to OTTAWA CAMP	
			arriving this about 1.30 pm.	APP. E.
OTTAWA	15		Coys at disposal of Coy Commanders	
CAMP.	16		The Battalion moved by march route to No. 1 AREA (DICKEBUSCH) at 8.55	
			am.	APP. F.
			Baths for battalion. 2nd Lieut A.C. GIBSON and O.R.R	
DICKEBUSCH	17		Patrol under Offr of Coy. B-y Coatage friendly a very useful initiale	
			Casualties — 4	

A6945 Wt. W14422/M1169 350,000 12/16 D. D. & L. Forms/C/2118/14.

Army Form C. 2118.

WAR DIARY
or
INTELLIGENCE SUMMARY.
(Erase heading not required.)

Instructions regarding War Diaries and Intelligence Summaries are contained in F.S. Regs., Part II. and the Staff Manual respectively. Title pages will be prepared in manuscript.

Place	Date	Hour	Summary of Events and Information	Remarks and references to Appendices
DICKEBUSCH.	18	2.30p	Battalion moved via VALLEY COTTAGES back to BEDFORD HOUSE	APP. G.
BEDFORD HOUSE.	19	8 pm	D° D° to position in JAM SUPPORTS.	No Casualties
	20	5.40a	Battalion advanced to the support, keeping close in rear of the 11th North Fus. All objectives were gained. Casualties (Killed) Nil. O.R. 41. Wounded O.B. Otr. 18? Missing O.R. 15. The wing of the Battalion was ordered at about 6.30pm, keep proceeding to TORK TOP TUNNELS.	
TORK TOP TUNNELS.	21		Battalion furnish carrying parties for the front line. About midnight Battalion proceeded to BEDFORD HOUSE. The remnant Officers and heavily were relieved by Officers from Reinforcement Camp and all men from Reinforcement Camp rejoined Battalion. Casualties 1 o.r. wounded.	
BEDFORD HOUSE.	22	At 5.30p.m	Battalion moved to Reserve position in SANCTUARY WOOD. Casualties - Lieut. Col. W.H. MIDDLETON D.S.O. wounded in face. Captain DORMAN-SMITH assumed command of the Battalion.	
SANCTUARY WOOD	23		Battalion furnish carrying parties (to front line. Casualties 2 o.r. killed 1 wounded	APP. H.
DICKEBUSCH	24		Battalion proceeded to N° 1 AREA (DICKEBUSCH) via KRUISTRAAT. Bands were Manned for the Batt?. Major H.L. LLEWELLYN assumed command of the Battalion. Casualties 5 o.r. wounded.	
	25		Battalion moved by march route to KENORA CAMP at 9.30 am. Captain E. TURNBULL joined the Battalion and assumed command of "B" Coy.	APP. I.

Army Form C. 2118.

WAR DIARY
or
INTELLIGENCE SUMMARY.
(Erase heading not required.)

Place	Date	Hour	Summary of Events and Information	Remarks and references to Appendices
KENORA CAMP.	26		O.C. Battalion inspected the Battalion at 9.30 a.m. Remainder of day spent in refitting, cleaning up etc.	
	27		Training etc. Bayts. paraded for inspection by the Divr. Gas Officer	APP. J.
	28		Battalion moved by march route to BROOK CAMP at 10.20 a.m.	
BROOK CAMP	29		Training etc. "B" + "C" Coys. moved to forward area at 4.30 pm to be employed by C.R.E. on forward roads.	APP. K.
	30		Church parade at 11.30 a.m.	

H. Stepherson Major
Commanding 10th Month. Fusiliers

APP. A

SECRET.
Copy. No....

BATTALION OPERATION ORDER. No.

1. The Battalion will move to PALACE CAMP, H.25.c.4.0. to-morrow.
2. Parade in lines ready to move off at 9-25 a.m.
3. Transport will move off with the Battalion.
4. All kit to be stacked by Transport Officer's tent by 8-30a.m.
5. Advance party consisting of 2/Lieut. E. ALLEN and 1 O.R. per Coy and H.Qrs., will report to Brigade H.Qrs at 8-30 a.m. They will meet at Orderly Room at 7-30 a.m.
6. All material borrowed from R.E. Dump must be returned before 8-30a.m. Each Coy will detail a senior N.C.O. to see that all material is stacked on the proper piles and not deposited in any order.
7. 200yds will be maintained between Coys.
8. ACKNOWLEDGE.

R.S. Bodger 2/Lt
Captain & Adjutant.
For O.C. 10th. Bn. Northumberland Fusrs.

2/9/17.

```
Copy No. 1. O.C. "A" Coy.
  "   "  2. O.C. "B" Coy.
  "   "  3. O.C. "C" Coy.
  "   "  4. O.C. "D" Coy.
  "   "  5. T.O.
  "   "  6. Q.M.
  "   "  7. R.S.M.
  "   "  8. C.O.
  "   "  9. War Diary.
  "   " 10. Office.
```

App. B.

Operation Orders.

1. The Batt. will march to the STEENVOORDE AREA to-morrow

2. Advance party consisting of Sec Lieut. H. G. B. Booth & 1 NCO per Coy. will meet at Orderly Room at 7.30 a.m. They will then proceed to Brigade HQ where they will report to the Staff Captain at 8 a.m.

3. Bn will parade on the open space near the entrance to the camp ready to move off at 1 p.m. Order HQ. D. A Band C. B
12.57

4. Transport will move with the Batt.

5. East of RENINGHELST 200 yds will be maintained between Coys.

6. First halt 1.47 warning march at 1.57 — Usual halts

1. All baggage & stores to be stacked at QM Stores by 12.30 p.m.

2. Dinners will be served before leaving camp at 11.45 am

Langley Davis
Captain & Adjutant
10th N.F.

2.9.17

O.C. A Coy
" B "
" C "
" D "
T.O.
Q.M.
R.S.M.

SECRET.   COPY NO......

BATTALION OPERATION ORDER NO.143.

1. The Battalion will move by march route to-morrow to
   H.Q. ROCHEFERNE AREA via OXELAERE-BAVINCOVE.

2. Battalion will parade ready to move off at 6-35a.m. Starting
   point LEEGISKAUK Estaminet K.33.a.2.9.   Order:-
   H.Q.,"B","C",.Band. "A",.& "D"Coys.

3. Transport will move separately, under the Command of Capt.H.HADDEN.
   A.S.C. to R.12.c.7.6.   Starting point K.39.d.4.0. Time 8-40a.m.
   Same route as above.

4. All baggage to be stacked outside Coy Headquarters at time of
   leaving and T.O. will arrange to collect same.

5. 2nd Lt.J.C. Ray. will be responsible for direction.

                                    ....Captain.
                                Adjutant.10th Northumberland Fusiliers.

Copy No.1.   "A" Company.
  "   " 2.   "B" Company.
  "   " 3.   "C" Company.
  "   " 4.   "D" Company.
  "   " 5.   Transport Officer.
  "   " 6.   Quartermaster.
  "   " 7.   C.O.
  "   " 8.   R.S.M.
  "   " 9.   War Diary.
  "   " 10.   Office.

4th September.=1917.

SECRET.   Copy No.........

BATTALION OPERATION ORDER. NO. 145.
----

1. The Battalion will move by march route to-morrow to STEENVOORDE (Central) AREA via BAVINCHOVE.

2. Battalion will parade ready to move off at 1-30 p.m. <u>Starting point</u>, Battalion Headquarters,.

    <u>Order</u>;- H.Q. "A","C",Band,"B","D" Coys.

3. Transport will MOVE separately under the Command of Capt.A.HADDEN. A.S.C.

    <u>Starting point</u>;- Road Junction, ZUYTPEENE.

    <u>Time</u>;- 1-0 p.m.

4. All baggage to be stacked outside Coy H.Qrs at 11-0 a.m. and Transport Officer will arrange to collect same.

5. Second-Lieut.P.L.DELANEY will be responsible for direction, and will report to Orderly Room to-morrow at 10-0 a.m. for instructions.

6. Strict attention will be paid to march discipline and a return will be rendered on arrival of all men falling out.

7. ACKNOWLEDGE.

    Copy No 1. O.C. "A" Coy.
    "   " 2. O.C. "B" Coy.
    "   " 3. O.C. "C" Coy.
    "   " 4. O.C. "D" Coy.
    "   " 5. Transport Officer.
    "   " 6. Quartermaster.
    "   " 7. R.S.M.
    "   " 8. C.O.
    "   " 9. Office.
    "   " 10. War Diary.

                    ....Captain & Adjutant.
    12th Sept.1917.   For O.C. 10th Bn. Northumberland Fusiliers.

App. E

SECRET.   Copy No..........

BATTALION OPERATION ORDERS... No.147.
----

1. The Battalion will move by march route to No.3.Area SHREWSBURY to-morrow.

2. Advance parties consisting of 2nd.Lt. J.W.GIBB. "A"Coy. and one O.R. per company and R.S. will report at the Square, SHREWSBURY at 6-30 a.m.

3. The Battalion will parade ready to move off at 8-25 a.m. the head of the column opposite "D"Coy's billet.
   ORDER:-   Band, H.Q., "D", "C", "B", "A".

4. All baggage to be stacked at Coy H.Qrs by 7-25 a.m.

5. The transport will move with the Battalion.

6. Breakfast will be at 7-30a.m. Sick Parade. 7-30 a.m.

7. ACKNOWLEDGE.

                                        Wrangley Davis
                                 ....Captain & Adjutant.
15th Septr.1917.   For O.C.10th Bn. Northumberland Fusiliers.

Copy No.1. O.C. "A"Coy.
  "   " 2. O.C. "B" " .
  "   " 3. O.C. "C" " .
  "   " 4. O.C. "D" " .
  "   " 5. Quartermaster.
  "   " 6. Transport Officer.
  "   " 7. R.S.M.
  "   " 8. O.C.
  "   " 9. War Diary.
  "   " 10. Office.

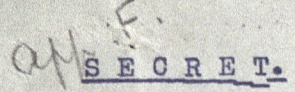

SECRET.   Copy No........

BATTALION OPERATION ORDER NO, 147.

1. The Battalion will move by march route to-morrow to No.1.Area.

2. Battalion will parade ready to move off at 8-55a.m. head of the column at entrance to the Camp.

3. <u>Order.</u> H.Q. "C","B",Band,"A", and "D" Coy. 100yds distance will be maintained between Coys.

4. All kit to be stacked at Q.M.Stores by 8 a.m.

5. Transport will move with the Battalion.

6. Breakfast 7-0 a.m. Sick Parade on arrival in new camp. Time to be notified later.

7. Advance party consisting of 2nd Lieut.E.Carr will proceed to and 1 N.C.O.per Coy & H.Q. take over the camp at 7-0.a.m.

8. ACKNOWLEDGE.

15th Septr.1917.   ....Captain & Adjutant.

```
Copy No.1. O.C."A"Coy.
 "   " 2. O.C."B"Coy.
 "   " 3. O.C."C"Coy.
 "   " 4. O.C."D"Coy.
 "   " 5. Quartermaster.
 "   " 6. Transport Officer.
 "   " 7. R.S.M.
 "   " 8. C.O.
 "   " 9. War Diary.
 "   "10. Office.
```

App. G.

SECRET.   Copy No. 7

BATTALION OPERATION ORDERS No. 148.

1. The Battalion plus two Coys of the 18th D.L.I. will move to BEDFORD HOUSE, parading ready to move off at 8-30 p.m.
   Order. H.Q., "D", "B", "A", "C".
   Platoons at 200 yards interval. Coys at 400 yds distance.

2. KIT. All kit to go back to Transport Lines will be stacked by the guard by 8-0 p.m. Greatcoats, haversacks, entrenching tools, etc, of men going into the line must be tied up in section bundles clearly marked and stacked with the other kit.

3. All Officers and men not proceeding to the line will after clearing the camp move back to the Transport Lines under the orders of Major.H.W.B.Foster.

4. The L.G.Limbers, one pack animal per Coy, and two for B.H. will accompany the Battalion to BEDFORD HOUSE. Four dixies per Company and two for Headquarters will be carried from camp.

5. At 9-0 p.m. the Battalion will move from BEDFORD HOUSE to YORK TOP. Order as before. Sections at 100 yds distance. Companys at 400 yds.

6. 2nd-Lt.STEWART. and 1 O.R. for B.Q. and Coys will proceed at 5-30p.m. to YORK TOP SUBWAY and take over the accommodation from the Town Major.

7. ACKNOWLEDGE.

                                                Chorley Davis
                                        ....Captn. & Adjutant.
16th Septr.1917.   for O.C. 10th Battn. Northumberland Fusiliers.

     Copy No. 1.   O.C. "A" Coy.
        "   " 2. O.C. "B" Coy.
        "   " 3. O.C. "C" Coy.
        "   " 4. O.C. "D" Coy.
        "   " 5. Quartermaster.
        "   " 6. Transport Officer.
        "   " 7. R.S.M.
        "   " 8. C.O.
        "   " 9. War Diary.
        "   "10. Office.

FILE/App H.

Operation Order.

1. Bn will move to-day to N of area DICKEBUSCH.

2. Advance party of Lt Thompson & 1 NCO per Coy & HQ will report to the Adjutant at 9.15 a.m.

3. Bn will start to move past HQ at 11.30 a.m. Order HQ D C A B.

4. Movement E of ZILLEBEKE will be by sections at 200 yds interval. W of ZILLEBEKE platoons at 200 yds.

5. Lt B Hallam, 2 NCOs per Coy & 1 NCO per HQ will remain behind to hand over positions on completion they will move to DICKEBUSCH.

6. Trenches & dugouts to be left clean & all latrines filled in.

7. Acknowledge.

Francis Davis Capt
Adjutant 10 NF

H.Q. 'J'

S E C R E T. 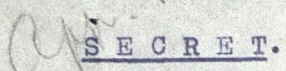 Copy No........

BATTALION OPERATION ORDERS. No. 149.

1. The Battalion will move by march route to-morrow 25th instant to KENORA CAMP (Sheet.28. M.3.c.8.5.) WESTOUTRE AREA.

2. Route LA CLYTE, WESTOUTRE.
   Time of Moving off 9-30 a.m.
   Order of March;- Band,H.Q.,"D",."C",."B",."A".
   Intervals of 200 yards to be maintained between Companies.

3. Transport will move with the Battalion joining the column at HALLEBAST CORNER. (H.32.d.8.1.)

4. Kits will be stacked at the guard room 8-30 a.m. The Transport Officer will also arrange to collect Signalling Equipment at that hour.

5. An advance party composed of 1 N.C.O. per H.Q. and Companies in charge of 2nd Lieut. Baker [R.A.DENT struck through] will proceed to take over the Camp on cycles to be obtained at Orderly Room, leaving at 8-30 a.m.

6. Sec-Lieut W.SWINDELL will be responsible for the direction.

7. Reveille. 6-30 a.m. Breakfast. 7-0 a.m. Sick Parade. 8-30 a.m.

8. ACKNOWLEDGE.

................Captain & Adjutant.
24th Septr.1917.   for O.C. 10th Battn. Northumberland Fusrs.

No.1.Copy. O.C."A"Coy.
No.2.Copy. O.C."B"Coy.
No.3.Copy. O.C."C"Coy.
No.4.Copy. O.C."D"Coy.
No.5.Copy. Q.Master.
No.6.Copy. Transport Officer.
No.7.Copy. R.S.M.
No.8.Copy. C.O.
No.9.Copy. War Diary.
No.10.Copy. Office.

App. I.

A.A.A.I.I.   Copy No......

BATTALION OPERATION ORDER. No. 180.

1. The 68th Brigade will move to-morrow, 11th N.F. and 15th D.L.I. to camps at HIGBY WOOD., Bde H.Q. 10th N.F. 12th D.L.I., 68th M.G.Co. 68th T.M.B. &1/1st Coy A.S.C. to camps in WESTOUTRE Area. (10th N.F. to BROOKE CAMP. K.10,d.7.1.).

2. The Battalion will parade on road adjoining football field ready to move off at 10.29 a.m.
   Order of March:- Band.,H.Q.,"A".,"B".,"C"."D".Coys.
   Transport will move in rear of the Battalion.
   Draft will parade with their Companies.
   XXX

3. Baggage will be stacked outside Q.M. Stores at 9-0 a.m., and C.?. "B" Coy will detail a loading party of 1 N.C.O. and 6 men.

4. Sick parade. 7-30 a.m. Breakfast 8-0 a.m. Dinner will be served on arrival in new camp.

5. 2nd-Lieut. T.F.SCRIPPS and 1 N.C.O. per Coy will parade at Orderly Room at 8-0 a.m. and will proceed to BROOKE Camp to allot tents etc.

6. ACKNOWLEDGE.

                                           E.G.Bodey.
                                           ....2nd Lt.Asst.Adjt.
27th Septr.1917.   for O.C. 10th Bn. Northumberland Fusrs.

Copy No.1. O.C."A"Coy.
  "   " 2. O.C."B" " .
  "   " 3. O.C."C" " .
  "   " 4. O.C."D" " .
  "   " 5. Transport Officer.
  "   " 6. Quartermaster.
  "   " 7. M.G.W.
  "   " 8. O.C.
  "   " 9. War Diary.
  "   " 10. Office.

SECRET.

Copy No _____

BATTALION OPERATION ORDERS No.191.

1. "B" and "C" Companies will move to the Forward Area this afternoon to be employed by C.R.E. on forward roads.

   Time of starting 4-30p.m.

2. Capt. TURNBULL will be in command.

   Route - Camp - Cross Roads - N.17.c.Central.- La Clytte.

3. They will report to Forward Area Commandant's office to pick up guide and tents.

4. Transport Officer will arrange transport to convey kit and stores to accompany these Coys, also two empty limbers to collect the tents at LA CLYTTE.

   Baggage to be at Transport Lines by 4-0 p.m.

5. Party will be rationed by 23rd Division after 30th. Rations for to-morrow will be taken with the baggage.

6. Cookers,one water cart and officers' chargers will accompany the party.

7. 2 Lewis Guns will be taken on limbers which will be unloaded and returned.

7. Party will return on Oct.2nd.1917.

8. ACKNOWLEDGE.

29th Septr.1917.

Langley Davis ....Captain & Adjutant. for O.C.19th Bn.Northumberland Fusiliers.

Copy No.1. O.C."B"Coy.
" " 2. O.C."C"Coy.
" " 3. Transport Officer.
" " 4. Quartermaster.
" " 5. C.O.
" " 6. War Diary.
" " 7. Office.
8 O.C. A Coy (for information)
9 O.C. D Coy (for information)

Army Form C. 2118.

8/3 /10 N F

26 R
1917

WAR DIARY
or
INTELLIGENCE SUMMARY.
(Erase heading not required.)

Vol 26

Instructions regarding War Diaries and Intelligence Summaries are contained in F. S. Regs., Part II. and the Staff Manual respectively. Title pages will be prepared in manuscript.

Place	Date 1917	Hour	Summary of Events and Information	Remarks and references to Appendices
OCTOBER			Fighting Strength O.R.R. 6 off. Ration Strength 29. 507	
BROOK CAMP.	1		Fighting Strength 41. 543 (incl "B" & "C" Coys.) Ration Strength 31. 557. Battalion (less "B" & "C" Coys.) moved by march route to the BERTHEN AREA. Returned in from lorries etc. at R.15.R. central.	APP. A
BERTHEN AREA.	2		Battalion (as above) moved by march route to THIESHOOK area at 12.30p Bivsd in farms. Battalion H.Q. at X.1.6.2.2.	APP. B
THIESHOOK AREA.	3		Training	
	4		Capt. W. ALEXANDER reported for duty from posted to "C" Coy.	
	5		D⁰. 2nd Lieu. I. F. WATSON d⁰. d⁰. "B.C."	
	6		Capt. E. E. DORMAN SMITH assumed command of the Battalion vice Major LLEWELLYN to Corps. Ref. Camp. Coys. on 40yds. range at X.1.6.1.2	
	7		Church parade. Lieut Col. W. H. MIDDLETON D.S.O. returned from Hospital and assumed Command of the Battalion. Captain E. E. DORMAN SMITH took over duties as 2nd in Command.	
	8		Battalion moved by march route to WESTOUTRE Area (BROOK CAMP - M.10.d.1.2.) at 8.10 am. arriving about 11.15 am.	APP. C
BROOK CAMP.	9		Cleaning up camp. Training. Battalion move by bus to SCOTTISH WOOD in the afternoon.	

Army Form C. 2118.

WAR DIARY
or
INTELLIGENCE SUMMARY.
(Erase heading not required.)

Instructions regarding War Diaries and Intelligence Summaries are contained in F. S. Regs., Part II. and the Staff Manual respectively. Title pages will be prepared in manuscript.

Place	Date	Hour	Summary of Events and Information	Remarks and references to Appendices
SCOTTISH WOOD.	10.	2.30 p.m.	Battalion moved to front line (2 Coys J.12.a.2.2., J.11.d.2.2., 2 Coys in Support at J.11. central. Batt. H.Q. THE BUTTE, POLYGONE WOOD).	
	11.		In the line.	
	12.			
	13.		Battalion was relieved on the night of the 13/14th inst. and proceeded to RAILWAY DUGOUTS.	APP. D
RAILWAY DUGOUTS.	14.		2nd Lieuts. J.F.EVANS and E.J.DRIVER reported for duty. "B" & "D" Coys. moved to Camp at N.2.b.2.7. (Ref Map. 28 N.W.)	APP. E
	15.		"A" & "C" Coys. moved to JOIST FARM AREA. Batt. H.Q. moved to Camp at N.2.b.2.7.	
	16.		Dispositions as above.	
	17.		" " "	
	18.		H.Q., "B" & "D" Coys moved at 10 a.m. by bus to the ECOLE to proceed to CLAPHAM JUNCTION to relieve 9th YORKS REGT. "A" & "C" Coys. moved from JOIST FARM to the BUND.	APP. F.
	19.		D⁰. " THE BUND to Camp at N.2.b.2.7.	
	20.		D⁰. moved by train from DICKEBUSCH to WIZERNES and then to	APP. G.

Army Form C. 2118.

WAR DIARY
or
INTELLIGENCE SUMMARY.
(Erase heading not required.)

Instructions regarding War Diaries and Intelligence Summaries are contained in F. S. Regs., Part II. and the Staff Manual respectively. Title pages will be prepared in manuscript.

Place	Date	Hour	Summary of Events and Information	Remarks and references to Appendices
	21		Billets at LONGUENESSE. "A" & "C" Coys. cleaning up billets etc. H.Q. & "B" & "D" Coys. were relieved by 1st EAST YORKS at CLAPHAM JUNCTION, and proceeded to Camp at 1.6.20.	APP. H.
	22		"A" & "C" Coys training-physical drill etc. H.Q "B" & "D" Coys. moved by bus to LONGUENESSE.	APP. I.
LONGUENESSE	23		Training & reorganization of Coys.	
	24		Training & reorganization of Coys.	
	25		Battalion paraded at 10.30 a.m. for inspection by G.O.C. 68th Bde.	
		2.30 pm.	Do. " " G.O.C. 23rd Div. and preservation of decorations.	
	26		Training	
	27			

Army Form C. 2118.

WAR DIARY
or
INTELLIGENCE SUMMARY.
(Erase heading not required.)

Place	Date	Hour	Summary of Events and Information	Remarks and references to Appendices
LONGUENESSE	28		Battalion on the Range at O.29.c.	
"	29		Practice for the C in C's inspection. L.O.C. 68th Bn. afterwards paraded antecedents of valour.	
"	30		Battalion started for the Range, but returned owing to very wet weather. Remainder of day spent in cleaning up, refitting equipment etc. for C in C's inspection	
"	31		Inspection by the Commander in Chief. Back for reinforcements at ST. OMER at 1 p.m. 2/in Battalion route march.	

Fighting Strength 36. 779 O.OR. Away from Unit 6. 75. Ration Strength O.OR. 31.704 Trench Strength 29.624.

M.A. Mickley Lieut Col
Commanding 10th North'd Fus.

App. A.

SECRET.   Copy No. 1....

BATTALION OPERATION ORDER. No. 152.

1. The Battalion (less "B" and "C" Coys) will move by march route to-day to the BERTHEN AREA.
   ROUTE:- Cross Roads - R.16.c.BERTHEN.

2. The Battalion will parade ready to move off at 2-0 p.m. Head of column facing H.Q. Mess.

3. Order:- H.Q., "D" Coy., Band., "A" Coy.

4. All kits etc wo be stacked at Quartermasters Stores by 12-0 noon.

5. Transport will move with the Battalion.

6. Dinner will be served at 12-0 noon.

7. Strict march discipline will be maintained throughout the march, and O.C. Coys will send a return to Orderly Room <u>immediately</u> on arrival, shewing the number of men who fell out enroute.

8. Sec-Lieut. E. WRIGHTON will be responsible for direction.

9. ACKNOWLEDGE.

E.E.Bodger 2. Lt. Captain & Adjutant.
For O.C. 10th Bn. Northumberland Fusiliers.

1st. October. 1917.

Copy No.1. O.C. "A" Coy.
Copy No.2. O.C. "B" Coy.
Copy No.3. Transport Officer.
Copy No.4. Quartermaster.
Copy No.5. R.S.M.
Copy No.6. C.O.
Copy No.7. War Diary.
Copy No.8. Office.

SECRET.   Copy No. 1....

SECRET. ~App. B.   Copy No.....

BATTALION OPERATION ORDER. No. 152.

1.   The Battalion (less "B" and "C" Coys) will parade ready to move off at 12-30p.m. on road outside Coy Billets.

2.   Order;- H.Q,. Band,. "A" and "D" Coys.

3.   All baggage to be stacked at Q.M. Stores by 11-0a.m.

4.   Dinner will be served at 11-30a.m.

5.   Sec-Lieut. McGUFFOG will be responsible for direction and will report to the Adjutant for instructions at 11-0a.m.

6.   Number of men falling out to reported to H.Q. immediately on arrival.

7.   ACKNOWLEDGE.

                                                        Captain & Adjutant.

1st. October. 1917.   for O.C. 10th. Bn. Northumberland Fusiliers.


```
Copy No. 1. O.C. "A" Coy.
  "   "  2. O.C. "B" Coy.
  "   "  3. R.S.M.
  "   " 4. T.O.
  "   "  5. Q.M.
  "   "  6. C.O.
  "   "  7. War Diary.
  "   "  8. Office.
```

SECRET. APP.C   Copy No. _____.

BATTALION OPERATION ORDER No.153.

1. The Battalion will move by march route to-morrow to No.8.Area
    WESTOUTRE.,S.W. (BROOK CAMP.) via BERTHEN-X roads, R.16.c.WESTOUTRE.

2. Battalion will parade ready to move off at 8-10a.m.
    <u>Starting Point</u>. LE ROOKLOSHILLE cross roads.
    <u>Order of March</u>. H.Q.,"A"Coy.,"B"Coy.,Band.,"C"Coy.,"D"Coy.

3. Transport will march in rear of Battalion.

4. Baggage will be stacked outside Coy billets at 7-15a.m. In the
    case of Officers baggage, this will be placed either with the Coy
    stores, or at the cross roads LE ROOKLOSHILLE, and Transport Officer
    will arrange to collect same.

5. Advance party consisting of 1.O.R. per Coy and H.Q., under Sec-Lt.
    H.F.W.KNOWLES, will parade at the cross roads LEROOKLOSHILLE at
    8-0a.m. and proceed to the new Area.

6. Strict attention will be paid to march discipline and a return
    will be rendered to Orderly Room immediately on arrival of all men
    falling out.

7. Sick Parade. 6-30a.m. Breakfast 7-0a.m.

8. ACKNOWLEDGE.

                                        _____Captain & Adjutant.
7th.October. 1917.   for O.C. 10th.Bn.Northumberland Fusiliers.

    Copy No.1. O.C."A"Coy.
    Copy No.2. O.C."B"Coy.
    Copy No.3. O.C."C"Coy.
    Copy No.4. O.C."D"Coy.
    Copy No.5. Transport Officer.
    Copy No.6. Quartermaster.
    Copy No.7. R.S.M.
    Copy No.8. C.O.
    Copy No.9. War Diary.
    Copy No.10.Office.

SECRET. App. D   Copy No. 6

OPERATION ORDER NO. 153.

1. **RELIEF.** The Battalion will be relieved by the 12th D.L.I. on the night of the 13-14th insts.

2. **GUIDES.** One guide per Battn H.Q. and one guide per platoon will meet the relieving Battn at the junction of the sleeper road and the duckboard track on 20th Bde track at 6-0 p.m. and will guide incoming Units to their positions. They will report to H.Q.(Bn) at 4-30 p.m.

3. **DESTINATION.** On completion of relief Coys will send an officer to report at Battn H.Q. and will proceed to Railway Dugouts.

4. **TRENCH STORES.** All trench stores, including tools, S.O.S. grenades, very lights, and bandoliers of S.A.A. taken over from relieved units, will be dumped at Battn and Coy H.Q. and handed over to incoming unit and receipt obtained.

5. **ACKNOWLEDGE.**

   N.B. Guides must be reliable men who know their way. The route from "A" Coy to Battn H.Q. will probably be marked by white posts before relief takes place.

12/10/17.
                                                   2/Lt. & Ass.Adjt.
                                     for O.C. 10th Bn Northumberland Fusiliers

Copy No. 1. O.C. "A" Coy.
"   " 2. O.C. "B" Coy.
"   " 3. O.C. "C" Coy.
"   " 4. O.C. "D" Coy.
"   " 5. C.O.
"   " 6. War Diary.
"   " 7. Office.
"   " 8. R.S.M.
"   " 9. T.O.
"   " 10. Q.M.

"A" Form.
MESSAGES AND SIGNALS.

Army Form C. 2121.
(In pads of 100.)

SECRET.

TO: C.C. A & C Coys.

Sender's Number: VS.36
Day of Month: 14

The above Coys. will proceed tomorrow (15th inst.) to JOIST FARM AREA to relieve two Coys. of 13th D.L.I.

Coys. will parade at 2.30 p.m. and will move to HOOGE CRATER where guides provided by the 13th D.L.I. will meet and conduct them at 3.30 p.m. to their position.

Rations for two days will be carried, and Coys. will collect sufficient water for their requirements when passing HOOGE CRATER.

East of HOOGE CRATER Coys. will move in small parties.

H.O.R. provided by "B" & "D" Coys. will accompany the party to their position.

"A" Form.
MESSAGES AND SIGNALS.

Army Form C. 2121.
(In pads of 100.)

TO { Communication

Sender's Number: BBA
Day of Month: 14
AAA

when they will return to Camp.
O.C. "A" Coy will report patrol
to Bde H.Q. by one of the four O.R.
previously mentioned.
ACKNOWLEDGE.

E.J Booker
2nd Lieut & Asst Adjt
15 Bn...

O.P.P.F.
SECRET

Operation Order No. 1.

1. The H.Q. and "B" & "D" Coys. of 10" N.F. will move this morning to CLAPHAM JUNCTION and will relieve the 9th YORKS REGT.

2. Busses will probably be available for the move and will report to Camp at 10 a.m. All men will debus at the ECOLE and march to CLAPHAM JUNCTION. A distance of 100 yds between platoons and 200 yds between Coys. will be maintained between the ECOLE and CLAPHAM JUNCTION.

3. Advance party already detailed will meet their respective Coys. on arrival at HOOGE CRATER.

4. All details will be left behind in present Camp.

5. The unexpended portion of the day's rations will be carried.

18/10/17

B.P. Snydam
2/Lt. & Adjt.
10 N.F.

SECRET.   Copy No....

BATTALION OPERATION ORDER. No. 156.

1. "A" and "C" Companies of 10th N.F. will parade ready to move off at 10-30 a.m. to-morrow.
   Order of March. "A" "C", in rear of 8th Yorks, and will entrain at DICKEBUSCHE at 11-30 a.m. and proceed to REAR AREA.

2. Transport will move under orders issued to Transport Officer.

3. Rations for to-morrow will be carried on the man.

4. Strict attention will be paid to march, entraining, and detraining discipline.

5. Officers kits, mess stores, and blankets will be stacked ready for loading at 7-0 a.m.

6. ACKNOWLEDGE.

                         E.G. Bodge 2/Lt. & Ass Adjutant.
                    for O.C. 10th Battn. Northumberland Fusiliers.

Copy No. 1. O.C. "A" Coy.
"   " 2. O.C. "C" Coy.
"   " 3. C.O.
"   " 4. Office
"   " 5. War Diary.

App. H

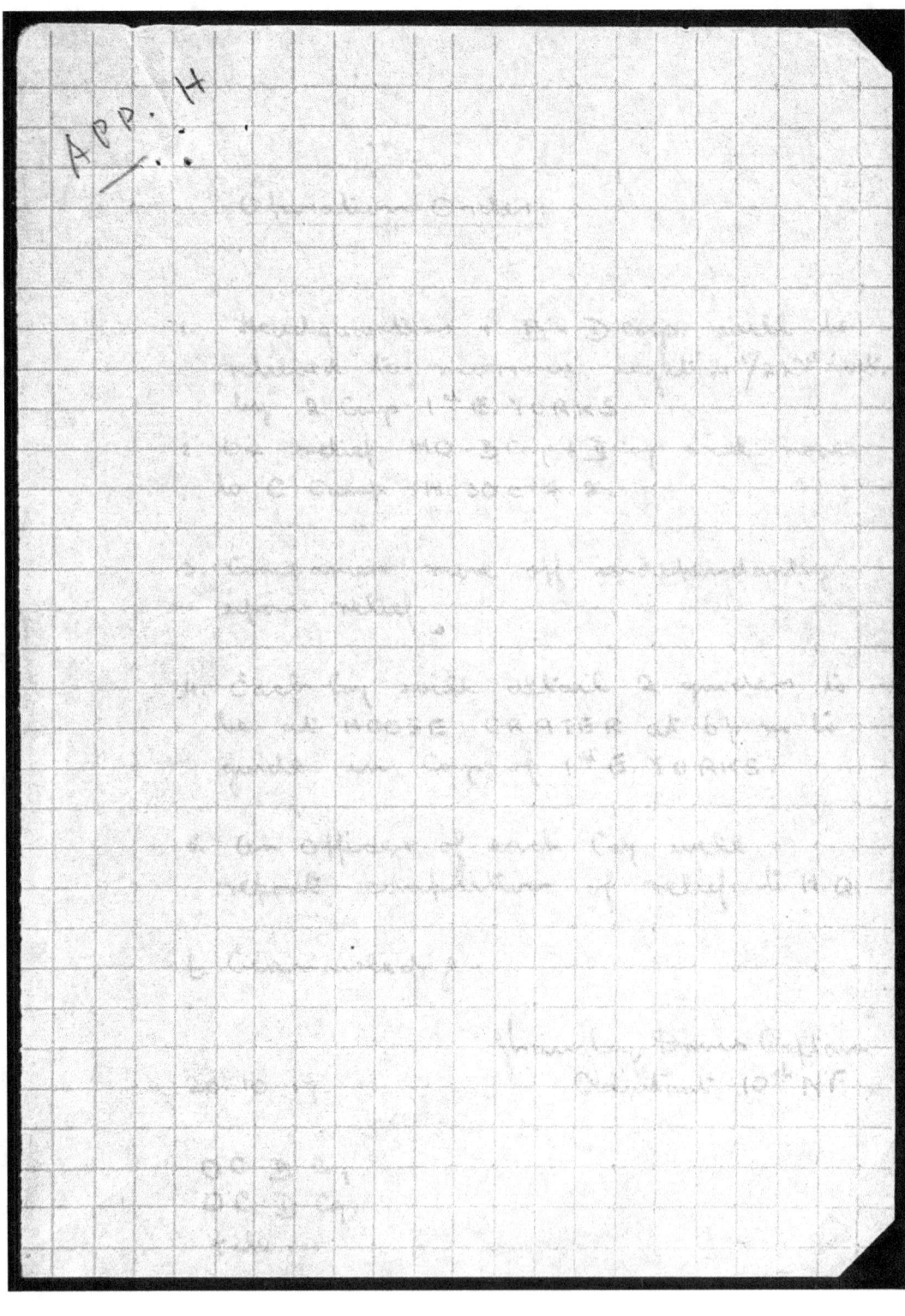

APP. 1.

www.ingramcontent.com/pod-product-compliance
Lightning Source LLC
Chambersburg PA
CBHW082006220426
43670CB00014B/2566